Learning That Lasts

Reflection Activities for Trainers and Designers

KATRINA KENNEDY

Alexandria, VA

© 2025 ASTD DBA the Association for Talent Development (ATD)
All rights reserved.

28 27 26 25   1 2 3 4 5

No part of this publication may be reproduced, distributed, or transmitted in any form or by any means, including photocopying, recording, information storage and retrieval systems, or other electronic or mechanical methods, without the prior written permission of the publisher, except in the case of brief quotations embodied in critical reviews and certain other noncommercial uses permitted by copyright law. For permission requests, please go to copyright.com, or contact Copyright Clearance Center (CCC), 222 Rosewood Drive, Danvers, MA 01923 (telephone: 978.750.8400; fax: 978.646.8600).

ATD Press is an internationally renowned source of insightful and practical information on talent development, training, and professional development.

ATD Press
1640 King Street
Alexandria, VA 22314 USA

Ordering information: Books published by ATD Press can be purchased by visiting ATD's website at td.org/books or by calling 800.628.2783 or 703.683.8100.

Library of Congress Control Number: 2025937429

ISBN-10: 1-960231-62-6
ISBN-13: 978-1-960231-62-8
e-ISBN: 978-1-960231-23-9

ATD Press Editorial Staff
Director: Sarah Halgas
Manager: Melissa Jones
Content Manager: Alexandria Clapp
Developmental Editor: Shelley Sperry
Production Editor: Katy Wiley Stewts
Text Designer: Shirley E.M. Raybuck
Cover Designer: Rose Richey

For Shea and Connor

Before you turn the page,
pause for a moment.

What do you hope to gain
from the pages of this book?

Contents

Foreword xi

Introduction xiii

Part 1. Reflection

   Chapter 1. What Is Reflection? 3

   Chapter 2. How to Add Reflection to Learning Experiences 13

Part 2. Activities for Learning That Lasts

   Chapter 3. Outcome 1: Boost Motivation to Learn 35

      Prior Knowledge Mental Inventory 40

      Quiz Me! 43

      Finish the Sentence 47

      I'm Curious About 50

   Chapter 4. Outcome 2: Build Social Connection 55

      Learning Maps: Reflections *on* Action, *in* Action 59

      Shared Learning Map 65

      I Would Title This 70

      Draw a Mind Map 73

      Reflect, Pair, Share 78

   Chapter 5. Outcome 3: Strengthen Memory 83

      Five Bullet Points 86

      One Question 89

      The Spinning Wheel of Wonder 93

      Fill In Your Box 97

      Draw Your Thought 101

      What's It Like? 105

Chapter 6. Outcome 4: Create Deeper Insight 109
    Take Two Minutes 111
    R&R 114
    Instructional Origami 118
    Four Corners 122
    Before and After 125
    What? Gut? So What? Now What? 128
    Wonder Wall 132
    Tell Me a Story 136
    Explain It to a Five-Year-Old 139

Chapter 7. Outcome 5: Assess Progress 145
    The Chat Cascade 147
    On a Scale of 1 to 5 150
    I Like, I Wish, I Wonder 153
    Just One Word 156
    I'll Use/Tell Me More 159

Chapter 8. Outcome 6: Improve Performance 165
    Insight and Action 167
    Start, Stop, Continue 170
    It's a RAP (Reflection Action Plan) 173
    Pause, Breathe, Think 177
    Just Imagine 180
    After-Action Review 183

Chapter 9. Outcome 7: Sharpen Critical Thinking 189
    Five Questions 192
    Plan, Monitor, and Evaluate 196
    What Went Well? What Could Be Better? 199
    If/Then 202
    Five Whys 205

Chapter 10. Outcome 8: Increase Self-Awareness 209
    Journaling 213
    The Coaching Conversation 216
    Your Best Experience 219
    What I Thought, What I Think 223
    Surprise, Failure, and Frustration 227

Conclusion 233
Acknowledgments 237
Appendix A. Activities at a Glance 241
Appendix B. Tools and Templates 251
References 271
About the Author 275
About ATD 277

Foreword

I first encountered Katrina Kennedy's work in training and talent development a few years ago at an industry conference in Orlando, Florida. We chatted for a bit over a cup of coffee, and I was immediately struck by the wisdom she shared and her depth of experience. She talked about learning transfer with equal parts passion and practicality. She also discussed reflection in a way that made me stop and think—exactly as she intended. I still think about that conversation today.

I've spent years writing about learning technologies, and I've seen many approaches come and go, but the power of reflection as a learning transfer tool has remained consistently undervalued—until now. Our ability to contemplate and learn from experience influences our future behavior. And Katrina wants to make sure we all understand that significance.

If you haven't yet heard Katrina's name, get ready. She's earned her spot in the list of L&D thought leaders with this well-researched and practical book. It's more than just a list of activities—it's a journey through methods you can use to promote retrieval and reflection. It's about how the power of the pause can take a training program from an event to a learning experience.

Katrina's almost 30 years of frontline experience in talent development spans across industries ranging from healthcare to technology. She has a remarkable ability to translate researched theories into accessible practice. What makes this book particularly valuable is its four-part model for progressive reflection, along with the seemingly endless list of questions it offers to help you use it. The book's reflection activities offer a refreshing take on learning transfer with practical methods you can use in any type of training program, whether it's in-person, virtual, or even asynchronous. You'll discover evidence-based techniques for adding reflection to learning experiences, boosting motivation to learn, building social connections, strengthening memory, improving performance, sharpening critical thinking, and more.

While it's hard to choose just one activity, the "Prior Knowledge Mental Inventory" technique described in chapter 3 particularly resonated with me. In fact, I recently used it in a virtual training program to help my participants uncover their prior knowledge and to help me fill in the gaps. It was a powerful experience for the learners and a useful tool for me as the facilitator. I also have plans to incorporate several other activities into future programs, including "Draw Your Thought at a Glance" and "Instructional Origami." This book is just so good—I can't wait to adopt many of the tools.

As you explore these pages, resist the temptation to simply grab techniques for immediate implementation. Instead, model the reflective practice that Katrina advocates by pausing after each chapter to consider when, where, and how each technique might fit best in your own learning environment. Katrina's thoughtfully included questions at the end of each chapter to help you jumpstart this process.

In today's fast-paced workplace, where professionals are expected to deliver measurable results with increasingly limited resources, the art of meaningful reflection has never been more important. As automation and artificial intelligence transform the way we work, our uniquely human capacity for reflection and insight will be our most valuable asset. Katrina's ideas offer techniques that honor the complexity of human learning while providing practical tools to facilitate it.

I can't think of a better guide for navigating this territory. *Learning That Lasts* represents the best of our profession: It's deeply informed by research yet grounded in the real world and, above all, it's profoundly useful.

Cindy Huggett, CPTD
Author, *The Virtual Training Guidebook,* 2nd edition
October 2025

Introduction

Whether you are responsible for training that covers safety procedures for aircraft mechanics or pivot tables for analysts, you've undoubtedly felt the pressure to engage participants. The training you provide is critical to their success and the success of your organization. Your mutual success can determine the safety of the public you serve as well as the longevity of your organization. Organizational learning is no simple endeavor.

Our jobs as trainers, facilitators, and instructional designers are more difficult than ever as we balance multiple priorities, limited time and resources, and the need to create engaging experiences that capture distracted minds. You may feel like you are fighting a losing battle.

Most lasting learning doesn't happen in a day or even a week, but we are sometimes given no more than that to help people gain the skills and competencies they need to be successful. Small adjustments to how we design and deliver learning experiences affect the success of mechanics, analysts, and the many other people we guide through learning experiences.

I wrote this book because I know how difficult it can be to take time to pause and reflect at work and at home. The world is moving faster, and expectations are higher than ever for those of us in the L&D profession. The need to hurry up, do more, and be better leaves us wondering: *Where did all our time go? How can we possibly make it through the intense demands we face every day?*

Reflection is one effective and meaningful answer to those questions. It is one of the things we can intentionally add to our training toolkit to help create lasting learning that transfers to our workplaces. Taking the time to reflect can outweigh additional practice in a well-designed learning experience—and it doesn't have to take long. Reflection can look like a few minutes spent discussing the valuable points of an activity. It can also look like two minutes spent writing down the key takeaways from an experience. It can happen in small groups, large groups, and individually. We can open training with "pre-flection," sprinkle reflection throughout, and then close with reflection. (*Reflectere* is the Latin word for "reflection." *Re* means "back," and *flection* means "to bend." *Pre-flection* simply means bending before we get started. This won't be the only word I make up.) We can also continue to support learning after training through intentional reflection check-ins.

Intentional reflection is woven into the fiber of my work and my being. Walk into my home and you will soon notice you're surrounded by photos of my family. Walk over to my bookshelves and you'll discover the books that inform and inspire who I am. If you happen to arrive when my family gathers for a meal, you'll hear me ask questions about everyone's day. The questions are meant to encourage a moment of reflection when we sit down to reconnect as a family. They help us pause to find the meaning and value in the day we've just completed. We create stronger family bonds, celebrate our accomplishments, and identify how we can support one another.

Everyone is so accustomed to my usual questions that my son, Connor, often starts asking them before I can open my mouth. And when I told my family that I wanted to write a book about reflection, Connor responded immediately, "Of course you do."

I use reflection to learn from my life experiences. I use reflection to help Connor maneuver life with multiple learning disabilities. I use reflection to remind my significant other about our to-do list. And, as you know, because you're reading this book, I use reflection in my work to help people learn more from their experiences.

For more than two decades, I've used reflection in my work as an instructional designer, a facilitator, and a trainer. At the beginning of training, I often ask participants to brainstorm everything they know to help them realize they know more than they think they do. I use debriefing conversations to help people think more critically about a topic we are exploring. I use "Chat Cascades" and "A Scale of One to Five" to add a touch of fun and lightheartedness to learning experiences and to fill gaps while waiting for a guest speaker to arrive. In emerging leader training, I've encouraged participants to reflect to increase their self-awareness and to develop a critical leadership practice.

In these pages, I share simple, practical tools and activities I've developed and tested over many years because I want you—and the people you influence—to discover the benefits of reflection.

Time to Pause

Reflection gives us the strategic pause we need to build more meaning in our lives, learn from our experiences, and make more thoughtful decisions. I can't think of a single instance when a pause, a breath, and a second to think doesn't improve outcomes.

This strategic pause is essential in our workplaces. Employees aren't clamoring for more to do; they crave more time for development, growth, and skill building. They long for meaning and connection. Put simply: They want a pause.

Fortunately, we can give people development and skill-building opportunities, meaning, and connection by helping them pause and reflect on their experiences in an intentional way.

Instructional designers, facilitators, trainers, managers—really, all of us—can benefit from a strategic pause to collect our thoughts, breathe, and see our next steps more clearly. I advocate for more reflection for everyone—including the people around my dinner table. But I'm addressing this book to my colleagues and friends in L&D—the instructional designers, facilitators, and trainers who want to create more effective, successful learning experiences.

We'll first discuss the basic questions of what reflection is and how you should consider using it. Then we will spend most of our time exploring specific reflection activities, engaging in the practice of reflection. Our profession is about performance, so we will focus on designing intentional reflection into our daily work through dozens of reflection activities—46 to be exact—each with a specific outcome.

It's true that anyone can reflect by asking one question: "What will I do with this experience?"

That question can activate many aspects of reflection to strengthen memory and, ideally, lead us to action. But isn't having a lot of choices better? Even if you prefer vanilla ice cream, wouldn't you like to know that you could choose chocolate or mint chocolate chip or another flavor if you were in the mood?

With that in mind, the book includes many flavors of reflection, each with a slightly different purpose, described in the outcomes. Some are vanilla, and some are a little more like rocky road. Trust me, though, these flavors of reflection come with no extra calories.

How to Approach This Book

You are free to choose your own adventure when reading this book. Start at the beginning and read each chapter in order, or turn to a chapter highlighting the particular outcome you need most and an activity or two that will work best with your approach to learning design and delivery.

The book opens with two short chapters that guide you through defining reflection and how to use it in learning experiences.

- **Chapter 1, What Is Reflection?** defines reflection and the science behind it, and introduces a reflection framework.
- **Chapter 2, How to Add Reflection to Learning Experiences,** outlines how to intentionally include reflection in your learning experiences.

At the heart of the book are eight reflection outcomes. Chapters 3 to 10 include activities you can use in instructor-led training, virtual instructor-led training, e-learning, and self-directed learning.

- **Chapter 3, Outcome 1: Boost Motivation to Learn,** focuses on helping people discover what they already know and why their experience is valuable.
- **Chapter 4, Outcome 2: Build Social Connection,** is about building and challenging participants' perspectives and insights through collaborative group work.
- **Chapter 5, Outcome 3: Strengthen Memory,** explores methods to strengthen neural pathways for better long-term retention.
- **Chapter 6, Outcome 4: Create Deeper Insight,** helps connect participants' existing knowledge to the new information in a learning experience.
- **Chapter 7, Outcome 5: Assess Progress,** is about checking in with participants, discovering how they are feeling, what they might need, and what they might be wondering.
- **Chapter 8, Outcome 6: Improve Performance,** focuses on strengthening participants' behaviors to develop their skills and enhance performance.
- **Chapter 9, Outcome 7: Sharpen Critical Thinking,** is about helping participants ask questions, draw conclusions, and analyze information.
- **Chapter 10, Outcome 8: Increase Self-Awareness,** is about participants discovering things they might not have realized about themselves.

Along with an explanation of each activity, you'll find a suggestion for the type of situation where it works best, a description of what to say and do, a way to make it more challenging, and a bit of a backstory on my experience with the activity. I provide details to support your facilitation skills, whether you are just starting out or are an experienced facilitator.

Each of these chapters also includes a list of questions you can use for reflection. These questions will help you work effectively with the energy of any group you are training. They can be used in place of or in addition to the activities.

Remember that you have many choices when you add reflection to your learning experiences. How you choose to approach reflection will depend on the outcome you hope to achieve. If you're designing a coaching program, you may want people to take time for self-reflection. If you want people to identify what they already know in compliance training, you might choose reflection to boost their motivation or deepen their understanding. You can use more than one outcome in a single program—or even try applying an activity for an outcome different from the one I suggest. Make each activity your own.

Your First Chance to Reflect

Before you turn the page, here's an initial activity to allow you to reflect on the following questions:

- What learning experience are you designing or delivering right now?
- What is one outcome you hope to achieve?
- Which chapter might help you achieve that outcome?

Thanks for pausing to go on this reflection adventure with me—I hope it benefits you now and well into the future. Please reach out if you have questions about anything I've written by contacting me through my website: katrinakennedy.com.

Read (and reflect) on!

-PART 1-
Reflection

Learning that Lasts is a how-to guide, but like most things, having a little background knowledge helps provide context and structure.

In part 1, we'll explore what reflection is and how to intentionally add it to your work. These chapters will help you create a deeper understanding of why many questions are worded in the way I've chosen to structure them. You'll discover why I avoid using "ands" and "ors" when formulating questions, as well as other methods to avoid bifurcating people's thinking.

I'll define many terms including *mental schema, rumination,* and *nostalgia. Bifurcation* and *metacognition* are the longest words I'll use—they are both really good words and the best ones to convey the ideas of splitting someone's thinking and thinking about thinking. More to come in the following chapters!

You'll also find a brief description of how the brain works and the benefits of reflection. While the neuroscience of learning is important for us to understand as learning practitioners, I'm leaving the deep science to those who are better equipped to dig into the intricacies of our brains.

Chapter 1 is filled with research and references to share with your manager when trying to justify the benefits of reflection. Chapter 2 will help you make sure you are getting the most benefit from time spent reflecting.

By all means, jump to part 2 if you are ready to dig into the activities. But I have a feeling you'll return to this section to find out why I rarely use adverbs ending in "-ly" in my questions and why you need to ask one question at a time. (Here's a hint, it's all about bifurcation.)

Chapter 1
What Is Reflection?

Change is the end result of all true learning.
—Leo Buscaglia, author and professor of education

My first job with a training responsibility was with the district attorney's Family Support Division. Like many of you, I was an accidental trainer, piecing together courses based on my previous learning experiences and trial and error.

I often asked groups, "How do you plan to apply what we've covered?"

Every time I've asked the question, I've noticed that participants remembered more and their questions became more complex. Course evaluations and on-the-job application improved. I didn't understand what was happening until I encountered the term *metacognition* in the 2002 book *Telling Ain't Training* by Harold D. Stolovitch and Erica J. Keeps. The authors gave me a label and an explanation for a phenomenon I'd witnessed in the training room. I needed to know more.

Stolovitch and Keeps define *metacognition* as "the set of higher-level (meta = above) control processes that guide our deliberate information processing activities." They identify five skills contributing to these processes, each of which relies on thinking about or reflecting on an experience:

- Planning to accomplish learning
- Selecting ideas
- Connecting ideas to existing knowledge
- Tuning old ideas with new
- Monitoring the understanding of ideas

You may have encountered other ways of defining metacognition, including "thinking about thinking" and "what we know about what we know" (Brown et al. 2014). But no matter how we define the process formally, we always come back to the incredible, transformative power of reflection.

Metacognition is reflection, and reflection is metacognition, but to keep things simple, I'll use the term *reflection* throughout this book.

What Happens When We Pause to Reflect?

We see the term *reflection* thrown around a lot on social media and in our work as L&D professionals. How many times a week do you read phrases like "I was reflecting on" or "Take a moment to reflect"? The term is used so much that it's become a platitude and has lost much of its true meaning.

This book is about reclaiming reflection and its capacity to enrich our learning experiences.

When we reflect, we look back on our experiences to reveal their meaning and value. Once we have discovered that meaning and value, we can better determine what our next actions should be, and our actions become more informed and intentional.

Over the past 20 years as a trainer, I've seen how reflection can change my professional direction and improve my well-being. Reflection has helped me make the right decisions in difficult situations inside and outside the training room. These may seem like big claims, but they are built on real-world evidence and practical experience.

Reflection isn't passive; it's about taking action. We pause. We think. Then, we decide what our experience means and what we can learn from it to move forward successfully. Reflection always includes the action we will take after we've considered an experience.

Giada Di Stefano and her colleagues describe reflection as an "intentional attempt to synthesize, abstract, and articulate the key lesson taught by experience" (Di Stefano et al. 2023). In other words, we are not just sitting back and ruminating on an experience. We are not engaged in nostalgia. We are intentionally processing what we've been through, identifying key insights, and expressing them in a way that makes them useful in the future. (We'll further explore rumination and nostalgia later in this chapter.)

Identifying key insights relies on our brain's ability to create neural connections. These connections form through a fascinating series of events in our brains. When we reflect on past events, the neural pathways used to create our memories are reactivated. Multiple brain regions, including the hippocampus, work together to reconstruct a memory. Then, the prefrontal cortex helps process this information to plan our future actions. No wonder reflection can make us tired! It consumes significant metabolic resources and can lead to mental fatigue. However, this effort ultimately creates stronger neural pathways, which lead to lasting learning. Interestingly, once these pathways are established, reflection can eventually free up energy in our brains by making certain thought processes more efficient.

How We Learn

Our brains are fascinating. We are always learning, whether we choose to or not. Our daily life presents opportunities for maneuvering through countless decisions. With each decision, a choice is made, and with that choice, we face a moment of committing the decision to memory or moving forward. When we take a moment to reflect on the decision, learning lasts. But what is happening in our brain?

Think about something that you can do without any support or aids. You might even say you are competent at the skill. Here are a few possible examples:
- Drive a car.
- Ride a bicycle.
- Cook a favorite dish.
- Access, read, and sort email.
- Facilitate a discussion.
- Solve a complex customer question.

If possible, recall how you got to the point you are at today. Where did you start? How did you feel? What means did you use to get feedback? How long did it take you to feel competent? How many times did you fail before you were successful? How did you learn?

Most people will say things like "trial and error," "a lot of practice," or "repetition, repetition, repetition."

When we encounter a new task or skill, we naturally compare it with our existing knowledge. Our brains seek context, connecting unfamiliar concepts to familiar ones through a process called "scaffolding." We build mental schemas, structures to help organize and link new information to our existing knowledge. You can imagine it as a bridge between old and new. As we learn, neural pathways form between existing and new knowledge. Through practice, trial and error, and feedback, these neural connections grow stronger.

> **MENTAL SCHEMAS**
>
> A mental schema is like an expectation. When you think of an elementary school classroom, you have a set of ideas or expectations about that classroom. You expect colorful walls, small tables and chairs, and noise when children are present. A classroom with adult-size desks and a mini-bar wouldn't fit your schema.

Spaced, varied, and interleaved practice create stronger neural pathways. *Spacing* provides practice over time, rather than clumping it all together. *Varied practice* refers to changing what we are practicing rather than repeating one thing over and over. *Interleaved practice* means we practice one thing, do something else, and return to the original practice. Add *retrieval* and *reflection* to all the processes discussed here and we've created conditions for learning to occur.

Spaced Repetition and Reflection

Before the COVID-19 pandemic, I provided an in-person, five-day, 40-hour course for new trainers and subject matter experts tasked with training. It was a lot of information spread over five consecutive weeks. I used spaced, varied, and interleaved practices with retrieval and reflection dispersed throughout. The course was effective. People remembered key points and were able to design and deliver training. But I overlooked an opportunity to make learning last.

During the pandemic (and after), I altered the course for the virtual environment, using three-hour segments stretched over 10 to 15 weeks. The difference was astounding. People learned more, asked deeper questions, and were able to perform more effectively than during the previous offerings. The only major changes I made were to the schedule and the amount of reflection. Reflecting at the beginning and between class segments was essential to success.

When we add reflection to our experiences, we can enhance our ability to learn and, in many cases, reduce our need for some practice. A research project led by Giada Di Stefano focused on newly hired employees and showed that time spent reflecting on a new skill was more beneficial to people than more time spent practicing that skill. The research team found that 15 minutes of reflection at the end of a training day led to a 20 percent increase in performance compared with spending that 15 minutes practicing and acquiring more experience (Di Stefano et al. 2023). This tells us that to gain the maximum learning benefit, we need to pair practice with time to reflect on our practice.

We've been told practice makes perfect, but it might be more accurate to say practice *and* reflection get us closer to perfect. As my friend, the community builder Anamaria Dorgo, has written, "We've been told a lie. Practice doesn't make perfect... It turns out that practice AND reflection make perfect" (Dorgo 2024).

Retrieve to Reflect

If I ask you to tell me your home phone number from when you were a child (or your parents' mobile numbers, if you are younger than 30), you must *retrieve* it from your memory. You can probably retrieve the number easily because, as a child, you dialed it so many times, getting it out of your head through the movement of your fingers. Today, smartphones have made it unnecessary for any of us to remember phone numbers, freeing up space for other important information—like where we left our phones.

Retrieval is the first step of reflection and involves calling information to the front of our minds to help create a long-term memory:

- When we ask someone to tell us three things they can recall, we are asking them to retrieve.
- When we give someone a quiz or test, we are asking them to retrieve.
- When I ask you to tell me the difference between reflection and rumination, I'm asking you to retrieve.

Retrieval is essential to learning. One way to distinguish retrieval from reflection is to think of retrieval as getting things out of participants' heads and reflection as asking them to think about the meaning of what they retrieved. They work closely together and are essential to forming lasting learning. Pooja K. Agarwal shares more about retrieval on a fantastic website, retrievalpractice.org.

Sometimes retrieval and reflection overlap. We will use both in most of the activities in this book. For example, you might be asked first to retrieve three things of value from your learning experience and then to reflect on how you'll use those things after training. You'll soon begin to appreciate their relationship to workplace learning:

Reflection → Learning → Behavior Change → Impact on Performance

Multiple Steps to Meaning

Reflection is a multistep process. We don't just ask people to sit in a meditative state for 15 minutes and expect meaning to emerge.

To gain the most value from our brains' efforts to create durable learning, we first need to break reflection into steps:
1. The first step uses activities to help people retrieve information about their experiences.
2. In the next step, we ask people to consider their feelings.
3. Then, we generate meaning from those experiences.
4. After we've identified meaning, we can determine our next actions.

Each of these steps takes time, but not an excessive amount. I'll define these steps with four questions you'll find repeated throughout the book:
- What happened?
- How do you feel about it?
- What was the value of the experience?
- What did you learn from the experience?

One other thing to note is that reflection activities can happen individually, in small groups or pairs, or even in a large group. You can also use a combination of group configurations with each step.

The Risks of Rumination

While riding my bike in my neighborhood on a busy Sunday afternoon, I almost ran into a pedestrian standing in the bike lane. No one was to blame for the series of events that almost led to the accident, but a gentleman standing nearby decided to tell me everything I'd done wrong. As I pedaled away, I was livid. For the rest of my ride home, I replayed his words in my head and my frustration grew, fueled by his misplaced judgment.

I didn't consider what I could do differently if the same situation happened again. I didn't rehearse responses for similar situations. I just replayed the event over and over and over. That, my friends, is the difference between rumination and reflection. Reflection would have taken me into the future. Rumination kept me mired in the past.

Reflection begins to slip into rumination when we focus on negative questions, such as (Kross et al. 2005):
- What went wrong?
- Who was at fault?
- Who or what is to blame?

We also slip into rumination when we beat ourselves up about choices that produced unexpected or unwanted outcomes. How often do you wish you'd done something differently and then berate yourself for your choices?

The healthy and productive alternative to rumination is reflection. Through reflection, we remain focused on future actions and try to learn from our mistakes instead of beating ourselves up over them. Unlike rumination, reflection allows us to discover new opportunities for growth and development.

Years ago, I witnessed the consequences of rumination while working on a strategic plan with a nonprofit board. I watched with growing concern as the board members focused on dissecting everything they'd done wrong to lose a large grant the previous year. Despite my efforts to move them toward reflection and action, they were determined to ruminate on their failures. They refused to learn from those experiences and move forward. Without a productive analysis of their processes, they missed opportunities available to them. They squandered their time and effort by placing blame, losing the grant for a second time. It is not an experience any facilitator wants to be part of.

Had they simply reflected on and responded to the question "What can we learn from this?" they would have moved forward to accomplish their goals.

The Nostalgia Trap

I love a good story. My father is a keen storyteller and always entertains me with his tales of growing up in the desert, riding motorcycles, and engaging in high school shenanigans. As he's gotten older, he's become more nostalgic, longing for days gone by.

Nostalgia is not reflection. Getting lost in nostalgia in the workplace can rob us of opportunities to innovate, collaborate, and grow.

Don't get me wrong. I'm not against nostalgia—I'm my father's daughter, after all. I often feel nostalgic about beloved books and can describe exactly where I was when I read them and what they meant to me. In a nostalgic mood, I will open those books and read them again to recapture those feelings, just like my dad will tell his stories again and again, finding comfort in the past. In a reflective mood, on the other hand, I will ask, "What did I *learn* from those books that I can apply in my life today?"

Nostalgia inspires us to long for our past, while reflection inspires us to learn from it.

Reflection Frameworks

Reflection is rooted in the Socratic method, developed in ancient Greece. Many of us learned the Socratic method in school, when teachers asked us a series of questions designed to ignite learning through discussion. The questions challenged our views of the world and deepened our understanding of the concepts we were debating. This questioning made us aware of our assumptions and helped us consider alternative perspectives. We learned.

Reflective frameworks, such as Driscoll's and Rolfe's models of reflection and Kolb's Experiential Learning Cycle, are similar to the Socratic method but take slightly different approaches to reflection for learning. What unites all these frameworks is that they try to make meaning from our experiences and create action from that meaning. They begin with a description of the experience followed by an analysis that leads to meaning. We can simplify any of the frameworks into four questions:

1. What happened?
2. How do you feel about it?
3. What was the value of the experience?
4. What did you learn from the experience?

I first learned to approach reflection through these four questions from Sivasailam "Thiagi" Thiagarajan, founder and resident mad scientist of the Thiagi Group, a training consultancy. He simply phrases the four questions as:

1. What?
2. Gut?
3. So what?
4. Now what?

What?

To answer "What?" or "What happened?," we describe our concrete experience. What did we see, hear, taste, smell, or touch? We discuss observable events. This question primes our brains for more difficult questions and helps us recall facts and details about our experience. It makes us pause to notice the details we often overlook.

This level of reflection is sometimes described as habitual or nonreflection, but it's a necessary question to ease us into deeper and more meaningful reflection. The "What?" questions might include:

- What did you notice about today's training course?

- What happened during that activity?
- What stood out to you about today's experience?

Gut?

"Gut?" or "How did you feel about it?" launches us into our *feelings* about an experience. What does our gut tell us?

Like the "What?" questions, there are no wrong answers for "Gut?" We simply need to acknowledge our feelings, our likes and dislikes, and our degree of difficulty, discomfort, or ease with our experiences. It's important to explore both the likes and the dislikes.

The "Gut?" questions might include:
- How did you feel about today's training course?
- What was difficult about this activity?
- What was easy about this activity?

In chapter 2, we'll discuss the importance of asking each of these questions separately to avoid bifurcating people's thinking.

So What?

The "So What?" question is the first reflective level in which we begin to explore the meaning of our experience. It is sometimes referred to as the first level of true reflection.

The first two questions—"What?" and "Gut?"—prepared us to go deeper. They primed our brains for more. "So What?" provides a reflective trigger, a moment when we naturally pause to consider the question. It requires more effort to respond to, making it much harder to answer than the first two questions.

Kolb's Experiential Learning Cycle labels this stage of reflection "abstract conceptualization," and we can see that it introduces an act of critical thinking (Hall 2023). We are creating a new idea about meaning from our concrete experience.

"So What?" questions might include:
- What did you learn from this training course?
- What was the value of this activity?
- What does today's experience reveal about your strengths?

Now What?

Now, we get to the action, moving from asking what we've learned to asking how we will use what we've learned in our daily work and life. This question is the most forward-thinking of the four as we identify future actions based on our experience. Kolb's Experiential Learning Cycle refers to this stage as "active experimentation." In this stage, the deepest reinforcement of learning occurs.

"Now What?" questions might include:
- What will you do when you return to work?
- What actions can you take after today?
- What specific changes will you make in the future?

These four questions—"What?" "Gut?" "So What?" and "Now What?"—are the threads binding all the activities in this book together. In the chapters that follow, you will discover activities for reflecting before, during, and after learning experiences. Many will rely on using the technique of retrieval before reflection.

Chapter 2
How to Add Reflection to Learning Experiences

> Between stimulus and response, there is a space.
> In that space is our power to choose our response.
> In our response lies our growth and our freedom.
> —Viktor Frankl, Holocaust survivor and author of
> *Man's Search for Meaning*

It's easy to throw the word *reflection* around when we're talking about creating our ideal learning experiences. It's challenging to dedicate sufficient time and space for meaningful reflection when designing or facilitating a class, especially with competing demands. I wish I had counted the number of times I've heard conference speakers say, "Take time to reflect on this," as they quickly move forward to the next topic or slide without a pause. As we've already discussed, there are powerful and important reasons to include a significant strategic pause for reflection in our learning designs and in our lives.

These are the questions I want to address throughout the rest of the book: How do we add those pauses to employee learning experiences? What are our options?

You might be tempted to add a reflection activity to the end of a class, hoping there will be time to include it. However, the time and mental space for reflection can shrink or disappear when participants ask more questions than you expect or you underestimate the time other activities will take.

We need a more intentional approach to reflection to ensure that everyone benefits from the process. This is why I advocate for designing with reflection in mind and helping people learn *how* to reflect.

In this chapter, we consider three questions about reflection in learning experiences:
1. How can we design the most effective reflection activities?
2. How can we successfully facilitate reflection practices?
3. How can we encourage ongoing reflective learning?

Design Effective Reflection Activities

From the start of the instructional design process, we need to give reflection the same importance as the content and cadence of our designs. This will make the process easier and ensure that the reflection itself is more effective for those who participate. First, make sure you understand the eight key outcomes (or benefits of) reflection (Figure 2-1):
1. Boost motivation to learn.
2. Build social connection.
3. Strengthen memory.
4. Create deeper insight.
5. Assess progress.
6. Improve performance.
7. Sharpen critical thinking.
8. Increase self-awareness.

Then, carefully align activities with learning objectives. Structure reflection activities before, during, and after a training experience, use open-ended questions, and set aside plenty of time. Above all, keep the people involved in your learning experience in mind as you select reflection activities.

Figure 2-1. The Eight Outcomes of Reflection

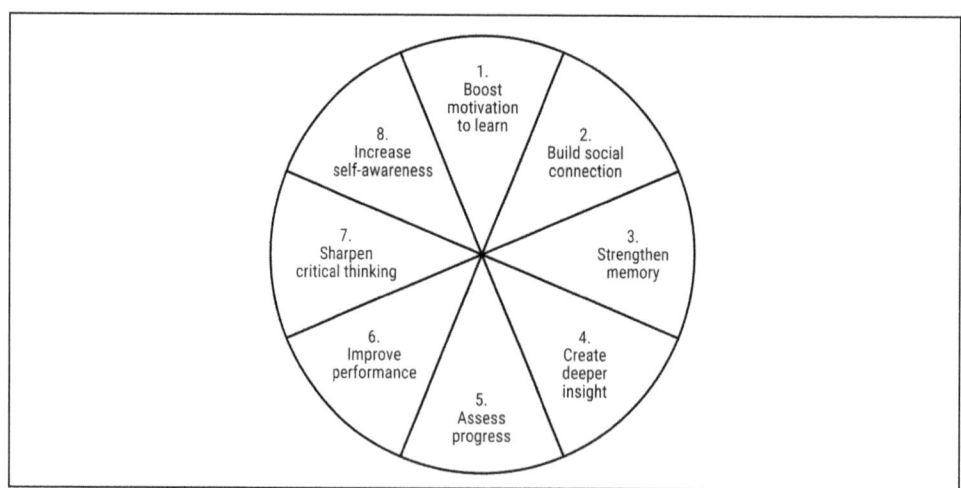

Know the Benefits of Reflection

Reflection does not come easily for everyone. As trainers, our challenge is to transform reflection from something participants do because it is on a required checklist into a practice they appreciate and desire because they know and value the benefits. To ensure that participants in our learning experiences fully understand the value of reflection, we need to clearly articulate those benefits, which I define as eight key learning outcomes. Chapters 3–10 examine each of the eight outcomes and provide practical, applicable activities for each.

> **REFLECT FOR A MOMENT**
>
> 1. What do you consider the value of reflection?
>
> 2. How would you describe the value of reflection to a friend or participant in a class you are facilitating?

Align With Learning Objectives

How do you determine how much reflection is correct for each situation? A good rule of thumb is if something is important enough to have a learning objective or outcome, it's important enough to have a reflection activity. In other words, use your learning objectives to determine how often to ask people to reflect. One learning objective? Include at least one reflection activity. More than one learning objective? Include more than one reflection activity.

A Four-Part Structure for Reflection

Consider beginning with reflection to identify what people know and what they want to learn. Then, include a short reflection activity after each objective. End with a culminating reflection activity focused on workplace actions. A typical structure for reflection might look like Table 2-1.

Table 2-1. Progressive Reflection

Reflection Timing	Reflection Question
First Reflection	What do you already know?
Objective 1	What do you want to use?
Objective 2	What was the value for you?
Final Reflection	What will you do when you return to work?

We will translate this general structure into activities in later chapters. Keep in mind that you have 46 activities to choose from and variations for each. The selection in Table 2-2 is just one example of a possible combination.

Table 2-2. Progressive Reflection With Activities

Reflection Timing	Reflection Activity
First Reflection	Quiz Me
Objective 1	Take Two Minutes
Objective 2	Five Questions
Final Reflection	Tell Me a Story

The more difficult a task or the more we require someone to change current behavior, the more time they will need for reflection. It's a straightforward sequence: Select your objective, match it to your intended outcome, choose an activity, allocate time, and repeat.

Select Objective → Match to Outcome → Choose Activity → Allocate Time

Ensuring that you have one reflection activity for each learning objective reinforces the most critical elements of your training program, helping to create durable and transferable learning experiences.

Structure Reflection Before, During, and After Training

How you, as an instructional designer or a facilitator, choose to structure reflection activities will guide a participant's learning before, during, and after a training experience. Set up an intentional structure for your content so you can ensure that your participants can better retain what they have learned and transfer those learning experiences to the workplace.

How often do you think about what you want to accomplish before a training event or an activity? I'll admit I'm not the best at reflecting before a learning experience. In fact, I often jump in with both feet only to discover I missed a few key details and need to regroup. But when I or the participants in my training courses intentionally stop to reflect before diving in, I've seen great results. Seeing participants' reflections before we begin to explore the topics gives me insight into adjustments I can make to the activities.

So, why not *begin* with a reflection—a moment to stop and ask the group to reflect on the question "What do you want to accomplish?" This can happen individually (without sharing) or in a group discussion.

Always ask yourself:
- Should participants reflect before, during, or after an experience?
- Or should they pause at all three points?

> **WISE WORDS ABOUT REFLECTION**
>
> Taking intentional time to write and "pre-flect" before a recent conference gave me more time to focus on which sessions to attend and what I was truly trying to accomplish. My session takeaways were much more relevant to my current projects and circumstances than if I had just gone to those sessions without more intentional pre-flection. I'll be adding this to my tool chest of other facilitation and debriefing strategies to use for learners in courses I develop in the future!
> —Sarah Crawford, ATD Member, Education Manager, and Learning and Development Consultant

In Table 2-3, you'll see that I recommend more reflection for people with less experience, but don't assume that means experienced participants need no reflection. Reflection at any time will benefit everyone, but the content and the participants' experience can help you determine your options.

Table 2-3. When to Reflect

Reflection Timing	Participants	Content
Before	People with some experience	Content like current experience or skill set
During	People with little experience	Multiple, complex topics
After	Everyone	Any content

Once you know where you will include reflection activities, you can explore the structure of your questions.

> **PAUSE TO CONSIDER**
> - How complex are the topics in your program?
> - How many reflection activities do you need for your program?
> - Where will you place them?

Use Open-Ended Questions

Questions are the heart of reflection. And better questions produce better reflection. As leadership expert and educator Amy Edmondson says in her 2023 book, *Right Kind of Wrong*, "A good question focuses on something that matters so we can think out loud together." I heartily agree. A well-formed question prompts deeper thinking and helps people reach the desired outcome.

Reflection in the learning experiences we design and facilitate often resembles the Socratic method discussed in chapter 1, which is widely used with students from elementary schools to university classrooms. The teacher asks a question, the student responds, and the teacher asks another question, pushing toward a deeper understanding of concepts and values. The best Socratic and reflective questions are open-ended.

Be warned, though—not every open-ended question is created equal. Consider the following two questions:
- What have you gained from reading this chapter?
- What's the best thing you've gained from reading this chapter?

Which question was easier for you to respond to? Do you notice the difference between the two? One word—*best*—in the second question makes it more difficult. The word *best* requires the person answering the question to engage in more thought and analysis of options. I suggest avoiding *most, least, best, worst,* and similar qualifiers unless there is a clear reason to narrow reflection to the best or worst of something. (You'll see an example of this exception in the Your Best Experience activity in chapter 10.)

Let's look at another set of open-ended questions. Pay attention to what happens in your brain as you read this paragraph:

> What did you like or dislike about the previous questions? Did they make you stop and think, or did they confuse you? Did you consider each one, or did you quickly move through them?

Did you pause to consider each question? If you're like most readers, you paused at the *and*s and the *or*s. The words *and* and *or* make one sentence ask two questions. Did you notice a moment of confusion? You need to make another decision with each *and* and *or*. Which question did you answer? The questions bifurcate your thinking, sending you in two opposite directions.

CRAFTING GOOD OPEN-ENDED QUESTIONS

What are the features of an effective open-ended question?
- They require more than a yes or no response.
- They prompt discussion and elaboration.
- They prompt more detail and explanation (unless you are talking to a moody teenager, who can manage a one-word, grumbled response to almost any question).

Try questions such as "What have you learned?" or "What was the value of this activity?" instead of questions such as "Did you learn something?" or "Was this helpful?" We can often make just a small adjustment to move a question from closed to open, as you can see in Table 2-4.

Table 2-4. Closed vs. Open-Ended Questions

Closed Questions	Open-Ended Questions
Did you meet all your deadlines this week?	How well did you manage your time this week? What were the challenges in meeting the deadlines?
Was this project a success?	What aspects of this project went well?
Are you satisfied with your workload?	How do you feel about the amount of work you have right now?
Do you feel comfortable asking for help when needed?	How do you feel about asking for help when needed?
Did you learn anything new this week?	What was something valuable you learned this week?
Did you have any frustrations this week?	What challenges did you face this week? How can you overcome these challenges in the future?
Did this exercise help you achieve the learning objectives?	What did you gain from this exercise?
Did you feel challenged by the new information?	What surprised you about the new information presented?

When we ask questions out loud, it's easy to do so in a rapid-fire series of run-on sentences that can confuse the person on the receiving end. When creating reflection activities, it's best to avoid asking a rapid series of questions, because people may register this as an interrogation. Ask one question, and then pause. Try to avoid multipart questions disguised as one question.

The bottom line—make it easier for people to respond:

- Ask one question at a time.
- Make them open-ended.
- Give people time to think.

Set Aside Adequate Time

Reflection takes time, but the time is worth it. You'll read some version of this statement in every chapter of this book.

Lack of time is one of the biggest obstacles to reflection. We all falsely believe we'll remember what's important and that we'll take time at some future point to review and reflect on our experiences. However, it's more likely that our future selves will find other things to do, neglecting the time to reflect.

We often lose our time to reflect in a learning experience because of excessive amounts of content. We have more to cover than our time allows, so reflection is the first thing to be eliminated. I experience this every time I go to a conference. I sit, listen, take notes, and then rush in my conference running shoes to the next session. I find my seat and repeat the same steps: Listen, take notes, rush.

More than once, I've arrived home (usually after a flight across a time zone or two) and reviewed my notes to discover I can't remember *anything*. The time and resources we spend attending conferences would be better invested if we'd all take the time during and after each session to reflect on our experiences and write down or discuss actions we'd like to take. I know better, yet I get caught in the same cycle again and again, and I suspect you do too.

> **REFLECT FOR A MOMENT**
> How will you ensure that time is incorporated for reflection?

Estimated Times for Activities

As you read through the activities in the following chapters, you'll find the estimated time to set aside for each activity. Use that as a guide when adding reflection to your projects. These guidelines are not hard-and-fast rules, so adjust all the times for your situation and participants. After you use an activity, make note of the time it required. Your notes will become a handy reference.

Facilitate Reflection

Once you've created a design with intentional, well-placed reflection, you can focus on how to facilitate reflection successfully. While you can always add reflection in the moment, meaningful reflection is easier when you've set aside adequate time and crafted your activities and questions with the participants and topic in mind. With the structure in place, you can explore how to make reflection work for everyone.

Help People Learn to Reflect

If the participants in your learning experience haven't spent much time *thinking about how they think*, the idea of reflection might be intimidating, so begin with something simple. Consider asking everyone to think of a meaningful life event—a birth, wedding, or first job, for example—and write down, in just a sentence or two, *why* it was so meaningful. They don't have to share it with you or anyone else. Most people will have no trouble recalling a meaningful personal event and explaining its value.

Once they've identified their individual moment, let them know that reflection during a learning experience is a lot like thinking about their everyday learning moments. You're asking, what's important here? Then, you're allowing a pause so people can consider why the moment was valuable. First comes the *pause* itself. Then comes the *thinking* about the significance of learning and how it affects actions.

After you've explained the value of reflection, it's time to guide people through how to reflect. Highlight the many options, including writing, discussing, and thinking individually and in small or large groups.

Reflection doesn't have to happen at a desk or in a training room. While there is value in written reflection, many people will also find value in reflecting while walking, exercising, or sitting in nature. Where reflection happens isn't as important as the act of reflection itself.

Answer the WIIFM Question

"What's in it for me?" (WIIFM) is the question every participant asks themselves at some point during a learning experience. If you can answer that question for participants or help them discover it for themselves, they'll be better prepared to reflect. A quick brainstorming activity can help reveal the ways that new information learned in a training program might be transferred to the workplace, for example. Asking people to identify challenges they face at work can help create a context for their experiences, leading them to better understand what's in it for them.

Create a Safe Space

Training can make participants recall previous educational experiences, and those may not always be positive. For many people, education was about producing the correct answers. This is one reason reflection can make people feel vulnerable. When we ask them to think about what they have gained from their experiences, they might feel compelled to provide the *correct* or *most acceptable* answers, instead of sharing their most honest answers. It's imperative that we create a safe space for training and reflection without sparking discomfort.

What does a safe learning space look like? It's a space where everyone can share their perspective without fear of judgment or ridicule. It's also a space where people have "the confidence that candor and vulnerability are welcome" (Edmondson and Hugander 2021). When we follow good reflection practices such as giving explicit instructions, including how reflection will be used and whether people will be required to share, we move closer to an environment where everyone can feel safe reflecting and sharing their reflections.

Give Explicit Instructions

People need and appreciate clear, direct instructions. They will experience less frustration and apprehension when you tell them what they need to do. For example:

- Where do you want them to reflect?
    - On paper?
    - In a shared digital document?
    - In an individual document they'll return to?
    - Within a learning management system?
- What questions are they asking or answering?
- Are they working alone or in groups?

If people are working in groups, consider assigning a facilitator to keep things moving and who can report back to the larger group. Most important, let participants know if they are going to be required to share their reflection or a portion of their reflection, or if it is private. To maintain trust with your group, do not change this requirement after you've announced it.

Limit the Focus

Let's consider two questions:
- What did you do last week?
- What did you do yesterday at work?

Which question is easier for you to answer? Although the answers to both questions might be tough to recall, most people find the second one easier to answer because it has a narrower focus with fewer things to consider before responding.

Narrowly focused questions or prompts can help participants engage in deeper, more meaningful reflection instead of spending most of their time trying to recall a lot of details.

The Power of Specificity

As part of narrowing the focus of your questions, be specific about details when you ask people to reflect. If you say simply, "Take two minutes to reflect," a typical participant might sit for two minutes wondering if they are supposed to reflect on the previous activity, the entire time you've been learning together, or some other moment.

When you introduce the moment to reflect, say instead, "Reflect on the previous activity." Or say, "Reflect on the last time you were in a difficult conversation." Framing your reflection in specifics helps everyone focus only on the point of the reflection.

A reflection activity can focus on an entire learning experience, a small moment, or a single activity. In any case, be direct and clear. You'll find that each activity included in this book gives you specific questions that you can adapt for your unique learning experiences and participants.

Sit With Silence

Once you ask a specific question, you need to pause. And wait. Asking reflective questions requires silence.

If you ask participants a question, sitting with silence can feel awkward as you wait for someone to fill the space between your question and their response. The time for people to respond will always feel longer for you as the facilitator than it will for the participants.

To fill the silent space, you can count backward from 20, squeeze your toes to give your energy somewhere to go, or take a strategic long drink of water.

Just wait.

Keep waiting.

Responses will arrive when you allow space for them. The larger the group you are reflecting with, the longer the silence is likely to be as everyone weighs the accuracy of their response, the security they feel in the group, and their confidence in their response (Figure 2-2).

Figure 2-2. Response Chart

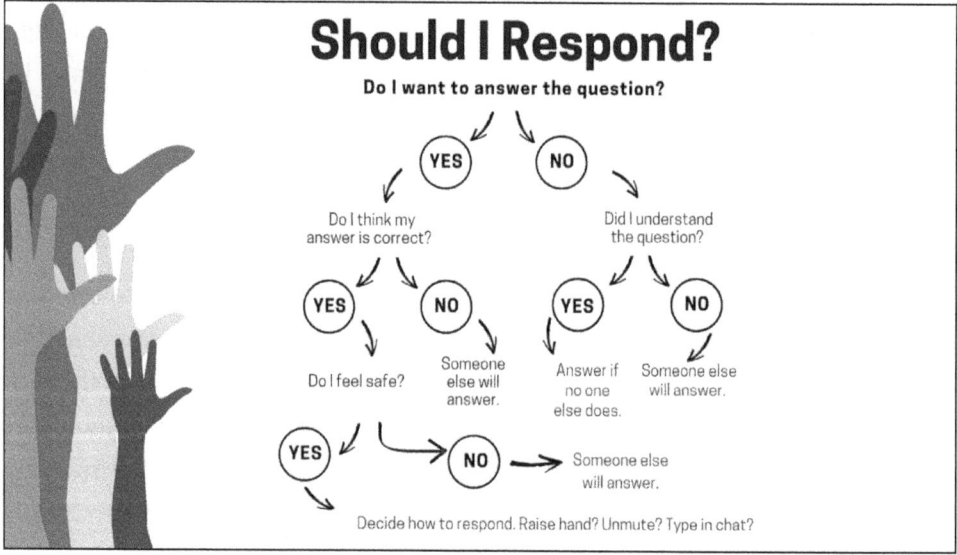

Make Reflection Work for Everyone

At this point, most of us are aware of the importance of designing for accessibility, inclusion, and belonging, although we don't do it perfectly in all cases. The tools and aids available to enhance the accessibility of both virtual and in-person training multiply each year.

Like all parts of learning experience design, we need to intentionally consider accessibility and inclusion when selecting and adapting reflection activities and methods.

Every person is unique, and their needs are diverse, but we can keep a few general considerations in mind for everyone. We can ask individual participants when we are unsure if we have made things accessible and inclusive for them.

We must communicate with participants to ensure that our options make learning accessible for all.

> **HOW WE USE PEOPLE'S INFORMATION MATTERS**
>
> My husband, Shea, is a high school environmental science teacher. Because we are both in learning professions, we enjoy comparing our experiences. Shea often attends staff meetings that include activities requiring him to share personal information in the interest of team building or icebreaking. He is often reluctant to participate and will refuse to take part when there isn't a clear explanation of how his information will be shared in the group.
>
> Shea feels no peer pressure to take part in something just because he's been asked, but that's not the case for everyone. Many people aren't that confident or comfortable bowing out of an activity.
>
> The lesson I take away from Shea's experiences is that I need to tell people in all my training programs how their reflections will be used. I need to answer the question, "Where are we going with this reflection?" Fully disclosing the intent of our activities when we begin helps everyone feel safer participating.

Providing options allows people to pick what works for them. You want each participant to reap the rewards of reflection, and flexibility in all your activities will benefit everyone. For example, I use the word *invite* throughout this book to encourage you to invite participants to take part in reflection, while not requiring it. In virtual training, I invite people to unmute to share their comments verbally or to add their thoughts to the chat. Adding private messaging or annotation can provide even more options.

In college, I was *required* to keep a journal for a sociology class. I had been journaling from the time I could hold a pencil, so it should have been a welcome activity. But knowing I was going to turn my journal in for a grade made me cautious, so the writing became stilted and awkward. I weighed every word I wrote carefully before putting it on the page.

If you want participants to be vulnerable and honest, and to get as much as possible from reflection, don't collect, grade, evaluate, or require reflection from anyone. The results will be more meaningful for them. Collecting journals won't entice a resistant participant to journal.

We need to provide options for reflection whether we are in person or in a virtual environment. Those options might include differences in the methods of reflection—handwriting versus typing versus speaking, for example. Or individual work versus group work. And, as I suggested, we should always provide options regarding whether participants will share their reflections. Let's explore these options in more detail:

- **Writing and recording options.** If an exercise asks people to write with a pen or pencil, also offer typing as an option. Voice-to-text might work best for other people, and in that case, you may need to offer a quiet space, such as a breakout room for virtual training or a private conference room for in-person training.
- **Individual, small group, or entire group.** Allow people to gracefully bow out of sharing anything they've reflected. What I'm comfortable sharing with one person might be very different from what I'm willing to share with 20 or 30 people. Always give people the opportunity to pass on sharing. Suggest they simply say, "Pass." I've watched many participants relax as soon as they know they aren't required to share what they've written. In my experience, no one appears to care when someone chooses to pass.
- **Movement—if it's available to you.** Do you want participants to move or stand for an exercise? Include "if it's available to you" as part of your directions for the activity. Allowing people to sit will avoid putting anyone in an awkward or dangerous situation in front of their peers, and this minor word adjustment will be appreciated.
- **Visualize or imagine.** Between 2 and 3 percent of the population cannot visualize images when you ask them to imagine something. Adding something like "if you are able to" or "if this is comfortable for you" to any set of instructions acknowledges those who can't or don't want to visualize something.
- **Close your eyes.** For many of us, closing our eyes when thinking or reflecting is a natural and comfortable response. For others, closing their eyes feels unsafe, placing them in a vulnerable position. Consider inviting people to close their eyes if they are comfortable. You could simply say, "Please close your eyes if that's comfortable for you." From time to time, I've noticed participants choosing to leave their eyes open. Their comfort is more important than my direction.
- **Acknowledge the energy.** Reflection can require significant mental and emotional energy. Some participants in an experience will lack the

energy to reflect, and it's best not to fight it. Lack of energy and lack of desire can look like the same thing, and as facilitators or trainers, we don't have a way to tell the difference. You can't force anyone into reflection, but you can make it OK for them to experience whatever they are experiencing. Acknowledging feelings can lead to our best reflection, because reflection is often about the feeling first.

- **Include all participants.** Take the time to adapt your reflection activities to ensure the inclusion of people who have physical or sensory differences or who are neurodivergent. You may never know if your adjustments benefit anyone, but that is the point. By default, you can make reflection more inclusive and help *everyone* who participates feel important and acknowledged without the need to call attention to themselves or to ask for anything additional they may need.

> **MORE WISE WORDS**
>
> What counts, in the long run, is not what you read. It is what you sift through your own mind; it is the ideas and impressions that are aroused in you by your reading. It is the ideas stirred in your own mind, the ideas which are a reflection of your own thinking, which make you an interesting person.
> —Eleanor Roosevelt, United Nations diplomat, humanitarian, and US first lady

Get Creative and Have Fun!

Reflection can be difficult, tiring, revealing, epiphanal, and mind changing. (I reflected on the use of *epiphanal*, and although it is not an actual word, I believe it should be. It fits the cadence of the sentence, and even though you won't find it in any recognized dictionary, I believe you'll know what it means.) But reflection can also be fun, creative, and invigorating. I hope you will have fun creating activities for the people you are working with. For example:

- Encourage light, easygoing approaches to reflection.
- Add colorful crayons, markers, and sticky notes to your toolkit, if they work for your group.
- Draw, dance, and move if that works.
- Get outside.

Take an unconventional approach whenever possible. And finally, remember that even if you have the time and space for only a short pause for intentional reflection, this will benefit participants much more than opting for no reflection.

Encourage Ongoing Reflection

Learning isn't confined to the time spent in a virtual or in-person training experience, and neither is reflection. We want to encourage and support ongoing reflection in a variety of ways. We can encourage people to add reflection to their daily practices, and we can provide reflection nudges through email, text, and other communications.

Encourage Participants to Review Previous Reflections

Reflection in the moment is valuable. The value increases, however, when we review reflection again after our initial reflection.

Encourage everyone to record their reflections in a place they can return to, such as a piece of paper, notebook, or computer file. Include multiple opportunities for reflection in your design and invite everyone to return to what they've previously written. Montclair University researchers Michele Rigolizzo and Zhu Zhu (2020) asked two workplace groups to reflect twice per week for eight weeks. They found that "the individuals who were able to see their previous reflections wrote significantly more subsequent reflections than the other group. In addition, those who could see their previous reflections used more words related to learning and cognition." Returning to our written thoughts becomes a powerful way to increase learning durability. It's essential to include revisiting reflections in programs aimed at developing self-awareness and behavioral change.

I asked people in an emerging leadership program to reflect throughout their multiple-week program. They reflected after each session and were encouraged to explore additional reflection questions when they returned to work. When they were asked to review their questions at the end of the program, they shared how their perspectives had changed and misconceptions they'd discovered about leadership. Most important, they shared about their own skill levels and readiness to lead. Their review of their reflections helped them see their progress. (I'll share what some people discovered in chapter 10.)

Encourage Systems for Ongoing Reflection

Invite everyone participating in a learning experience to continue their reflective practice afterward. You can support ongoing reflection by providing prompts through text or email reminders or system notifications. You can also consider researching chatbots or text response methods to provide prompts for reflection.

Shannon Tipton (2023), chief learning officer of Learning Rebels, encourages what she calls "drip feeding." This is "a method of delivering learning lessons in broken-up and timed increments [that] reinforces the concept of spaced learning and increases the likelihood of knowledge retention and application." A drip-feed approach, using chatbots or email, can also work for reflection.

Another way to support ongoing reflection is by bringing people together after a learning experience in person or virtually. Invite them to share reflections developed since the program's completion. Involving managers in this process can increase impact and transform learning from a one-time event to an ongoing experience.

You can also explore reflection applications that send notifications reminding people to take a moment to reflect on their learning experiences. I've listed several in the recommendations at the end of the book.

Reflect on How You Use Reflection in Designs

Think about how you are using reflection in your course designs. Is there adequate reflection? Are you explaining the value, purpose, and benefits of instruction?

Use this list to review how you are using reflection and determine the areas in which you can add or adjust reflection:

- I've created a safe and supportive learning environment where people feel comfortable sharing their reflections and engaging in open discussions.
- I've explained the value and benefits of reflection.
- I've identified if reflection will be shared with others when I explain the activity.
- I've included structured reflection activities to encourage thinking critically about experiences, assumptions, and actions.
- I've used a variety of reflective activities with different modes of reflection (written, verbal, and visual).
- I've aligned activities with the course outcomes or objectives.
- I've provided multiple opportunities for reflection throughout the learning experience.
- I've provided clear prompts or questions to guide participants' reflection processes.
- I've provided multiple means for ongoing reflection after completion of the learning experience.

- I've included opportunities for collaborative reflection, such as group discussions or peer feedback sessions, to encourage diverse perspectives and learning from others.
- I've considered the diverse needs of people.

QUIZ: LET'S REFLECT!

Ready to explore reflection activities? Before you dive in, let's test your knowledge of reflection for learning. The answers to the questions are on the next page.

1. What is one benefit of reflection?
    a. Boosts motivation
    b. Increases work speed
    c. Improves typing skills

2. When is it beneficial to reflect?
    a. Only after completing a task
    b. Before, during, and after an experience
    c. Once a year, during performance reviews

3. What are two obstacles to reflection?
    a. Excessive content and lack of time
    b. Too much sleep and exercise
    c. Quiet environments and comfortable seating

4. Which learning principle is often closely tied to reflection?
    a. Rote memorization
    b. Speed-reading
    c. Metacognition

5. What is metacognition?
    a. A type of meditation
    b. Thinking about thinking
    c. A learning disability

6. What improves reflection over time?
    a. Writing with a pencil and paper
    b. Only reflecting on positive experiences
    c. Practice and structured activities

QUIZ ANSWERS: LET'S REFLECT!

Remember, missing a question might just help you create a more durable memory! Let's review the answers to the quiz questions.

1. A benefit of reflection is that it boosts motivation (a); 2. It is beneficial to reflect before, during, and after the experience (b); 3. Two obstacles to reflection are excessive content and lack of time (a); 4. Metacognition is the learning principle that's most closely tied to reflection (c); 5. Metacognition is thinking about thinking (b); 6. Practice and structured activities improve reflection over time (c).

How'd you do? Did you miss some? Learning takes time. Come back a little later and try these questions again. For now, turn the page and head into the activities. I hope you enjoy them.

PART 2
Activities for Learning That Lasts

In chapters 3 through 10, you'll find activities grouped according to the eight outcomes discussed in chapter 2. You may read each chapter sequentially or go directly to the outcome that best fits the learning experience you are designing or delivering. Each activity includes:

- A brief introduction about the science behind the activity or additional background information
- An easy-to-read table (At a Glance) showing key information about the activity, including the reflection type, instructional format (virtual instructor-led training, instructor-led training, e-learning, or self-directed), group size, suggested time to complete, and when to perform the activity (before, during, or after)
- A short description of the activity
- Step-by-step instructions and a facilitator's guide showing what to say and do during the activity
- Several ideas to help you increase the value of the activity
- A version of the activity (Try It for Yourself) that you can try before using it with other people
- A description of exactly why I like the activity

I've provided three distinct sets of instructions for each activity to support you, no matter your level of knowledge or experience. The format may appear repetitive but is intended to provide guidance for each activity in a format that best meets your needs. Some people will prefer step-by-step instructions, others will like the format of the guide, and still others will just want to glance at the short description. Use whatever format works best for you.

Appendix A includes a table to help you select the activities that best meet your needs.

Chapter 3
Outcome 1: Boost Motivation to Learn

Finding out that you are wrong is even more valuable than being right because you are learning.
—Amy Edmondson, author, *Right Kind of Wrong*

Have you ever had to do something you didn't want to do? Who hasn't been there, right? What motivated you to do the thing? Was it a potential consequence? The threat of losing something or someone? How did you gain the confidence to do the thing you needed to do?

Years ago, I worked with Marcus, a state of California employee responsible for painting the Golden Gate Bridge. He'd been given the task of presenting orientation information to new employees. The idea of speaking publicly—especially to his peers—terrified him. Yet he could comfortably hang 746 feet in the air suspended by a few slim lines of safety equipment.

We began to discuss Marcus's work, hoping to come up with a solid plan to help him get through the presentation. We discussed the confidence he had in his painting, and he mentioned a safety checklist he references every day before beginning his job. He shared how valuable his checklist was. After a quick moment of reflection, we were able to create a presentation checklist. This brief reflection, combined with the detailed speaking checklist, helped calm his initial fears. Practice would help him overcome the rest.

Boosting people's motivation to learn is no easy task, but it's important in any learning experience. Harold Stolovitch and Erica Keeps (2002) note that "adults come to a learning situation with their own priorities and attitudes. They are ready to learn when they decide to open their minds and spirits to it." In this chapter, we will discover activities to help create that open-minded readiness.

Motivation and Curiosity

Let's explore why motivation is important and how we can improve it with reflection when engaged in a learning experience. One way learning designers and facilitators often try to motivate participants is by asking questions. Let's try a few. Don't look these up—just take a guess. (Answers are at the end of this chapter.)

1. What is the capital of Denmark?
2. Who wrote the first Gothic horror novel?
3. What is the square root of 64?

How many answers did you know right away, without much thought? How many questions did you think about for a moment, take a guess, and then move on from? Did a question stump you? And if so, did you feel an urge to look it up? Are you curious about the answer? I'm guessing the question you found hardest might have boosted your motivation to learn. During training, we typically ask a set of questions directly related to the training topic, always including an easy question and one hard enough to boost motivation to learn.

In a training session to help subject matter experts design learning content for their peers, I asked three true-or-false questions to spark participants' curiosity:

1. People learn best in a single, preferred learning style (such as visual, auditory, or kinesthetic). True or false?
2. A good night's sleep helps consolidate memories, improving learning. True or false?
3. The more difficult something is to learn, the less likely you are to remember it. True or false?

Participants were intrigued and motivated when their answers were incorrect. The questions appeared easy, but the answers were unexpected. We had a lively discussion about the myth of learning styles and how our job as trainers is *not* to make things easy, but to find the point of desirable difficulty for each participant. The use of true-or-false questions forces everyone to pick a side. And in case you're wondering, only the second statement is true.

Not every person we work with will be motivated to learn, but simple curiosity frequently drives our motivation to learn. Consider how often you pick up your phone to look up a random fact. These days, our devices feed our curiosity constantly, inviting us into the next funny reel, the next pretty post, the next tidbit of surprising or enraging information.

As L&D professionals, we use the power of natural human curiosity to motivate people to learn. Reflection can help by validating and activating what people already know, which will be the topic of all the activities that follow in this chapter. These kinds of reflections have several other beneficial results, including reducing discomfort with a topic, increasing people's interest in closing performance gaps, and creating a positive, accessible, and inclusive learning environment.

> **A FORMULA FOR MOTIVATION**
>
> Researchers have found that reflection boosts our belief in ourselves. When we believe in ourselves, our motivation increases (Di Stefano et al. 2023). I think of it as a powerful formula:
>
> Reflection → Confidence → Motivation to Learn → Learning → Performance
>
> When people reflect on what they bring to a learning experience, they may experience a greater sense of belonging. The person who thinks, "I can do this. I fit in this environment," is better prepared and more motivated to learn. They are experiencing a sense of acknowledgment and belonging.

Validating and Activating Prior Knowledge

When people reflect on what they *already know*, it can entice them to add to their knowledge and skills. When we activate prior knowledge through reflection, we allow people to connect ideas that already exist in their knowledge banks to brand-new ideas. I often begin training by asking everyone to take a few moments to list what they know about a topic. They show their existing knowledge, and I can acknowledge their experience.

As instructional designers, by honoring existing knowledge, we help create more readiness for learning. For example, we can ask participants to think about problems they've faced related to the training topic. A question as simple as "What has your experience been with this?" acknowledges people's past experiences in a way they usually appreciate.

After being diagnosed with dyslexia at age nine, my son struggled with self-confidence. He became reluctant to learn. After watching his teachers try everything to engage him for months, I had an idea. Together, he and I created a four-page list of everything he already knew how to do—his prior knowledge—including running, sword fighting, playing video games, and building with Legos. I watched his confidence and attention in school and at home increase as his list grew. Ten years later, we still reference and laugh about that list.

Increasing Interest in Closing Gaps

We are all more motivated when we are aware of our knowledge and skills gaps. Research across nursing, medical school, and leadership studies has demonstrated this phenomenon (Ribeiro et al. 2018). In one study, students watched a video highlighting unfamiliar aspects of an initially unmotivating topic. After viewing, they expressed an increased interest in learning. This shift in awareness is often referred to as the *curiosity gap* (Ditta et al. 2020).

By encouraging people to reflect on knowledge gaps at the start of a learning experience, we boost motivation throughout. Knowledge pretests demonstrate this well. A pretest helps people identify their gaps, motivating both curiosity and focus. In the Training for Trainers program I offer, groups work through a short pretest together at the beginning of each day. The pretest includes review questions about upcoming content, allowing participants to reflect on their learning and preview upcoming objectives.

Creating a Positive, Accessible, and Inclusive Learning Environment

The actions we take at the beginning of training set the tone for everyone's success. Acknowledging existing experience creates an inclusive learning environment and leads people to share their perspectives and ask questions more readily.

Measuring prior knowledge also creates a more accessible class because this measurement helps us identify and close gaps in knowledge, which is essential for success.

Reflection activities often reveal important participant needs. During one What I Already Know activity, a participant noted their use of closed-captioning for hearing difficulties. This prompted me to turn on PowerPoint's closed-caption feature for the duration of our program. I now always default to the use of closed captions for in-person training and events.

Before you review the activities in this chapter, take a moment to consider when you need to help boost people's motivation to learn in your training programs.

A Pause for Designers and Facilitators

Think about a learning experience that you anticipate designing or delivering soon. Considering these questions will help you select an activity that best fits participants' needs:

- Who are the participants?
- What do they already know?
- How will you acknowledge their existing knowledge?
- Are they reluctant or ready for your learning experience?

> **A REFLECTION BOOST FOR MOTIVATION**
>
> As trainers and facilitators, we aren't always prepared with the perfect reflection activity. In a pinch, you can use the following questions if you want to add a quick pause for reflection to a learning experience. The questions might be enough to reenergize or refocus a group.
>
> Choose one or two questions for a quick boost to motivation:
>
> - What do you already know about this topic?
> - What do you want to know about this topic?
> - What do you want to be able to do after class?
> - What prompted you to participate today?
> - What do you want from this experience?
> - What are your fears about this learning experience?

Activities

This chapter's activities will help participants in your learning experiences reflect on their existing knowledge to boost their motivation to learn. You'll notice that most are in the category of Reflection Before Action and can be revisited during and after a learning experience.

Prior Knowledge Mental Inventory

With this activity, you help people identify what they already know, prime them for the next training topic, and boost their motivation to learn. People's motivation increases when they share their existing knowledge and skills and receive recognition from the facilitator. The Prior Knowledge Mental Inventory also provides facilitators with insight into participants' backgrounds.

To create a Prior Knowledge Mental Inventory, ask participants to list everything they know about a topic or an idea. People can work alone and then share ideas with the group, or they can create a group list.

AT A GLANCE

Reflection Type
- Individual response, publicly shared
- Small group response, publicly shared
- Large group response

Instructional Format
- Virtual instructor-led training
- Instructor-led training
- E-learning
- Self-directed learning

Number of Participants
- Any number

Time Needed
- 2–3 minutes for individual reflection
- 8–10 minutes for group reflection

Reflection Timing
- Before

The Activity

Ask everyone to write down absolutely everything they think they already know about the topic you are about to cover. Set a timer. Announce when time is up and conduct a debrief.

Step-by-Step Instructions

1. Ask everyone to think about the topic.
2. Set a three-minute timer.
3. Ask them to write everything they know about the topic.
4. After three minutes, ask them to stop.
5. Form groups of three to five people.
6. Invite each group to write five to seven of their ideas in a shared space, such as on a whiteboard or paper chart.
7. Encourage duplicates, highlighting ideas, and reorganizing.
8. When each group's list of ideas is complete, ask what participants notice about the ideas they've gathered.

9. Discuss:
   - Concepts that align with what you are going to cover
   - Areas that weren't mentioned
   - Any misconceptions
10. Dive into your topic, inviting everyone to reference their individual and group's list as you move through your time together.

Facilitator's Guide

What to Say	What to Do
Let's see what you already know about today's topic. In the next three minutes, I'd like you to write everything you know about [*the topic*]. Ready? Go for it!	Set a 3-minute timer.
It has been three minutes, so please finish the thought you are on. It turns out you know a lot about our topic, don't you? Now, let's combine our knowledge.	
Everyone, please gather in small groups of three to five people. Write the information you came up with on a virtual whiteboard [*or paper chart, if in person*]. It's OK if you duplicate answers.	Form groups of 3 to 5 people.
Now, work together to underline what you believe is the most important information about our topic.	Monitor groups to ensure understanding.
In your small groups, discuss what patterns or new ideas you see in the information.	
What did you notice about the ideas you've gathered?	

How to Increase the Value

- Return to the Prior Knowledge Mental Inventory as you move through your program, highlighting the items you've covered.
- Create a competition by asking groups of three to five people to write their inventories together. As you move through your topic, invite people to place check marks next to each idea as it is covered in class. At the end of your program (or time together) ask everyone to total their check marks, lobbying for checks when ideas they've listed are close but not exactly what was covered. Cheer for the group with the most checks!

Why I Like This Activity

I start most of my Training for Trainers programs by asking participants to write down everything they would do if asked to design and deliver a learning experience. I request they start with a verb to mimic the task analysis process they will learn as we tackle analyzing training needs. The task analysis outlines the tasks and steps performed on the job, and it's a critical part of good instructional design. You'll notice most of the activity steps I've provided are written this way.

I love to watch a screen or a large space on a classroom wall fill with everyone's ideas. It's so helpful for people to see their existing knowledge as well as the group's collective knowledge. There are always duplicates, missing concepts, outliers, and even a few learning myths listed. After the exercise, I pay attention to any gaps to guide the training program going forward.

Give It a Try

Set a three-minute timer. In the space provided, collect items for your Prior Knowledge Mental Inventory.

Here's everything I can recall about the value of reflection.

NOW ASK YOURSELF

- When could you use a Prior Knowledge Mental Inventory?
- Which groups would this work well for?
- How could you alter this activity to fit your specific program and participants?

Quiz Me!

Quizzes can help us learn and motivate our curiosity. They can be a source of reflection on what we know, what we don't yet understand, and what we need to learn to move forward. Used strategically and thoughtfully, quizzes help us gain insight into our learning process and strengthen our memory.

Quizzes at the beginning of a program help reveal what people already know and what they don't know. Research shows that pretests can increase retention and later recall even when people don't have any prior knowledge (Yang et al. 2020). Low- or no-stakes testing is critical for reducing test anxiety and ensuring successful knowledge retention. The quiz method I'm suggesting here is low stakes and not graded.

Keep in mind that you don't have to call this activity a quiz or a test. Get creative! Make the activity work for your participants. Maybe the terms *Wisdom Warm Up*, *Insight Inventory*, or *Knowledge Check* are better for your environment.

AT A GLANCE

Reflection Type
- Individual response, private
- Individual response, shared anonymously

Instructional Format
- Virtual instructor-led training
- Instructor-led training
- E-learning
- Self-directed learning

Number of Participants
- Any number

Time Needed
- 5–7 minutes recommended
- Note that time will vary based on the number of questions included

Reflection Timing
- Before

The Activity

Write three to five multiple-choice quiz questions. Use your course objectives to help write the questions. Give participants the quiz, explaining that it helps them identify what they already know.

These content-specific questions can help prime participants for learning and increase the durability of learning throughout their experience.

Step-by-Step Instructions
1. Provide everyone with a set of quiz questions about the content being covered.
2. Aim for questions that stretch participants but are not so difficult that they can't get some right.
3. Write the questions based on your learning objectives.
4. Conduct the quiz.
5. Provide the answers.
6. Remind everyone that there is no expectation to know all the answers. They will gain the knowledge in your time together.

Facilitator's Guide

What to Say	What to Do
Let's see what you already know about our topic. We're going to take a quick quiz with just a few questions. You may know some of the answers, and you may not know others. That's OK. This is low stakes, and it's not going in your HR file! Research suggests that a quiz will help you retain information longer. Here we go.	Provide the quiz in a digital or print version.
	Set a timer. Watch participants for signs they are finished. Adjust time as needed.
How did that go for you? Which questions are you curious about?	Respond to any questions about the questions.

How to Increase the Value
- Consider using the game-based learning platforms Kahoot! or Slido for a fun quiz variation.
- Ask participants to write quiz questions for their peers throughout a program or after a multiday experience. Give them a format to follow with a few examples. Use these questions to start programs or as quick reflective reviews. I love saving the questions that classes produce to use in future classes or to alter my delivery.

- In her 2021 book, *Write Better Multiple-Choice Questions to Assess Learning*, Patti Shank recommends crafting effective questions by precisely stating what's being tested, using plausible distractors, and avoiding negative phrasing or complex language. I agree!
- Use an artificial intelligence (AI) assistant such as ChatGPT or Claude to help you write quiz questions. You'll need to experiment to find the best approach to writing prompts.
- Here is an AI prompt I use:

Generate a set of [*number*] multiple-choice questions on [*specific topic or skill*] for a multiple-choice quiz. Write the questions for adults at a [*grade*] reading level. For each question:

- Write a clear, complete stem that precisely states what's being tested.
- Provide one correct answer and three plausible distractors.
- Use positive phrasing and simple language.
- Include an explanation for the correct answer.
- Ensure the questions cover key concepts and learning objectives for [*specific topic or skill*].

Why I Like This Activity

Early in my career, I met a challenging participant who told me and everyone near him that he knew everything we were going to cover and could teach the class himself. He was self-assured and a bit condescending.

When the quiz started, this participant was suddenly silent. His eagerness to impress us was replaced by a humble realization that he didn't know what he didn't know. He was far more receptive for the remainder of our time together. I'll admit it was gratifying to witness his humbling transformation.

QUIZZES AS MEMORY AIDS

In their classic 2014 book on learning, *Make It Stick*, authors Peter C. Brown, Henry L. Roediger, and Mark A. McDaniel refer to testing as "retrieval of learning from memory." You could also use the Quiz Me activity to help with outcome 3, Strengthen Memory.

Give It a Try

Select one answer for each question. You'll find the correct answers at the end of this chapter.

1. What is one of the benefits of reflection in learning experiences?
   a. It increases the speed of content delivery.
   b. It strengthens neural pathways for better memory retention.
   c. It eliminates the need for practical application.
   d. It reduces the time needed for instruction.

2. How should time be allocated for reflection activities in course design?
   a. Save reflection for the end of the course.
   b. Limit reflection to under five minutes per session.
   c. Plan for dedicated reflection time in your course structure.
   d. Use reflection only when extra time is available.

3. Which question helps spark the reflection process?
   a. What stands out for you about reflection?
   b. What was the most beneficial thing you've learned about reflection?
   c. When will you use reflection?
   d. Do you like reflection?

NOW ASK YOURSELF

- When could you use Quiz Me?
- Which participants would this work well for?
- How could you alter this activity to fit your specific program and participants?
- What challenges do you need to consider when using Quiz Me?

Finish the Sentence

Reflection frameworks benefit people who are reluctant to reflect. Finish the Sentence is a framework to help people identify their existing knowledge and reflect on their goals and anticipated obstacles in a learning experience. When they complete the framework, they can ask for peer support to increase the value of their work. Think of Finish the Sentence as workplace Mad Libs with more purposeful choices.

AT A GLANCE

Reflection Type
- Individual response, private
- Individual response, publicly shared
- Small group response, publicly shared

Instructional Format
- Virtual instructor-led training
- Instructor-led training
- E-learning
- Self-directed learning

Number of Participants
- Any number

Time Needed
- 8–10 minutes

Reflection Timing
- Before
- During
- After

The Activity

Provide everyone with a series of incomplete sentences related to your topic. By completing the sentences, participants will reflect on what they want to accomplish in the learning experience. This helps people get specific about their expectations, wants, needs, and obstacles. The framework can be adapted to a variety of topics.

Step-by-Step Instructions

1. Acknowledge that participants arrive in class with knowledge of the subject.
2. Ask each individual to consider what they already know and what they want to achieve by completing each sentence.
3. Provide everyone with enough time to complete the sentences.
4. Ask everyone to share their sentences using one of the following methods:
    - Form small groups of three to five people.
    - Ask for volunteers.
    - Post in a shared location to view and discuss.
5. Ask what everyone noticed about the sentences.

Facilitator's Guide

What to Say	What to Do
	Before the session, prepare slides or a handout with an incomplete sentence or series of sentences related to your topic. They could include: • Accessibility is: • Coaching is: • When we provide feedback, we: • Leadership is best described as: • We learn best when we:
I know you know something about our subject today. Research shows that reflecting on what you know before we start will help make your learning more durable.	
Let's take a few minutes to reflect on what you know already and what you hope to gain today.	
Fill in the incomplete sentences with words or ideas that best fit your thoughts and experiences.	Share the sentence-completion slide or document.
You have 10 minutes.	
Wrap up the thought you are on.	
Let's form groups of three to five people to share your frameworks. Know that you can say, "Pass" if you don't want to share a portion or any of what you wrote.	Form groups of 3 to 5 people. If in person, consider using color-coded stickers or name tents to quickly create groups.
Let's come back together now. Thank you for sharing with your group.	
Save your list; we'll return to it at the end of our time together.	

How to Increase the Value

- **In person:** Post the incomplete sentences to chart pages. Invite everyone to write their responses on the charts or on sticky notes that they then attach to the charts.
- **Virtual:** Create a shared whiteboard, document, or online bulletin board like Padlet where everyone can share their sentences.
- If you gather a large number of responses before launching a program, consider using an AI tool, such as Claude or Gemini, to identify trends and common themes in the responses.

Why I Like This Activity

Finish the Sentence provides a structure that makes it easy for everyone to reflect and for me to compare everyone's responses. I can quickly see what everyone needs from class. When I used this technique during the kickoff of a five-week Training for Trainers program, seeing participants' responses before we began allowed me to connect with them personally and tailor the curriculum to better meet their needs.

Give It a Try

Let's consider your thoughts on being an emerging leader in your organization.

Finish the Sentence: Emerging Leadership

- ☐ I want to be a leader to _____.
- ☐ When I think of leadership, I think of _____.
- ☐ Managing people reminds me of _____.
- ☐ When I'm done with this program, I hope I can _____.
- ☐ One obstacle I anticipate is _____.

NOW ASK YOURSELF

- When could you use Finish the Sentence?
- Which participants would this reflection work well for?
- How could you alter this activity to fit your training course?

I'm Curious About . . .

There is comfort in leaning into our curiosity. It's usually safer for people to explore what they are curious about than revealing what they don't know. This activity helps people reflect on what they want from a learning experience.

The I'm Curious About activity relies on sentence completion, making it similar to the Finish the Sentence activity. In this case, a longer series of related statements is provided for reflection throughout the program.

Here's a short example of how someone might fill in the blanks in this activity:

> I am curious about *how I can improve my well-being* because I want to find out (what/how/why) *I get overwhelmed with my work priorities* to better understand (what/how/why) *coping skills for work and for home* so I will be able to *focus on my family and give them the time I'd like*.

AT A GLANCE

Reflection Type
- Individual response, private
- Individual response, publicly shared
- Small group response, publicly shared

Instructional Format
- Virtual instructor-led training
- Instructor-led training
- E-learning
- Self-directed learning

Number of Participants
- Any number

Time Needed
- 3–4 minutes for individual reflection
- 10–12 minutes for group reflection

Reflection Timing
- Before

The Activity

This activity provides a framework for participants to reflect on what they want to achieve from an experience. The guided framework makes reflection easier for those who might be reluctant to reflect. Return to this activity during and after the experience. Participants benefit when they can return to the work they previously completed. Also consider providing a completed example.

Step-by-Step Instructions

1. Give everyone a template with the incomplete sentence.
2. Provide an example to help get people started.
3. Ask them to take 10 minutes to complete the sentence.

4. At the 10-minute mark, or when everyone appears ready, ask participants to complete the thought they are on.
5. Invite everyone to post their work in a shared space.
6. Ask everyone to review their writing at the end of your time together.

Facilitator's Guide

What to Say	What to Do
Something prompted each of us to be here today. You arrived with something you are curious about and something you want to be able to do after class.	
I'm going to provide you with a framework to consider. Fill in the blanks with your perspectives.	
Here's my example. Yours will be different of course.	Show example: *I am curious about how to engage participants because I want to find out what grabs their attention to better understand why I'm losing people so I will be able to lead a more engaging virtual training.*
Now it's your turn. Please fill in your curiosity statement.	Monitor the group and clarify any questions.
Please wrap up the thought you are on.	
We'll return to these at the end of our time together.	Conduct training.
Now that we are wrapping things up, find your curiosity reflection.	Show your example as a reminder of what they are looking for.
Take a few minutes to read what you wrote. Add any additional notes or thoughts.	
Optional: Get in small groups. Share your responses to these questions: • What surprised you about your initial responses? • Did you already know what you were curious about? • What else do you need or want?	Post the questions where everyone can see them. Clarify any questions and monitor progress.

How to Increase the Value

- Invite everyone to place their reflections in a shared location in the room or on a shared document if working virtually. Allow people to opt out of sharing.
- Return to the I'm Curious About . . . activity at the end of your program. Ask everyone to complete a new set of prompts like the following ones. This time, they should reflect on the experience they have completed.
    - And now I know that _____
    - means I need to _____
    - so I can _____
    - My challenge will be _____

Why I Like This Activity

This activity provides a rich view of what people want to explore during class and achieve after class. It's a great resource for us as facilitators, and it also helps participants frame what they hope to gain. Returning to the activity later in a class or program helps reinforce learning, reminding everyone of their original goal.

Give It a Try

If you're giving this one a try, I would suggest considering what made you curious about the topic of reflection in general or this book specifically.

I'm Curious About Reflection

I am curious about _____

because I want to find out (*what/how/why*) _____

to better understand (*what/how/why*) _____

so I will be able to _____

NOW ASK YOURSELF

- When could you use I'm Curious About . . .?
- Which participants would this reflection work well for?
- How could you alter this activity to better fit your specific training event?
- What curious phrases might work for your training?

Conclusion

Not everyone is ready to learn or reflect. Some people require a little more support—or even prodding. I suggest using reflection to create readiness to learn.

When people reflect on what they already know about a topic, the act of reflection boosts their motivation. This boost is important for reluctant participants, those who are not confident in their skills, or anyone who doubts their knowledge. Participants begin to identify what they know, and trainers and facilitators are able to acknowledge people's past success with learning. In short, a well-chosen reflection activity helps people look back to prepare them to move forward by activating their prior knowledge.

This chapter explored reflection activities that boost participants' motivation. Each helps reduce people's discomfort with a topic, increase their desire to close performance gaps, validate what they already know, and create a positive, accessible, and inclusive learning environment. The activities included:

1. **Prior Knowledge Mental Inventory:** A quick brainstorming activity that collects everything known about the topic to acknowledge existing knowledge
2. **Quiz Me:** A multiple-choice-quiz method to identify knowledge gaps before training to increase curiosity and desire to learn
3. **Finish the Sentence:** A purposeful version of a Mad Libs activity to discover learning expectations and needs
4. **I'm Curious About . . . :** A fill-in-the-blank activity identifying what people want to learn and what they will do with their new knowledge

For the facilitator, the activities also reveal knowledge and skills that people already possess, helping them tailor the learning experience more precisely.

FINAL QUESTIONS FOR REFLECTION

Think of a learning experience you anticipate designing or delivering soon and reflect on how you might boost motivation.

- Which of your learning experiences would benefit from reflection to boost motivation?
- Which motivation-boosting activities best fit your training?
- What modifications do you want to make to any of the activities?
- What are you wondering about boosting motivation?

ANSWERS TO CHAPTER 3 ACTIVITIES

Boost Motivation Answers

1. Copenhagen is the capital of Denmark.

2. Horace Walpole wrote the first Gothic horror novel—*The Castle of Otranto*—in 1764. Many people guess the answer is Mary Shelley. However, while Shelley's *Frankenstein* was the first Gothic horror novel to swap a monster or man for a creature that was the "embodiment of human folly, brought to life through the power of science," she didn't invent the genre (Pagan 2018).

3. The square root of 64 is eight.

Quiz Me Answers

1. Reflection in the learning experience strengthens neural pathways for better memory retention (b).

2. Ensure there's time for reflection activities by including dedicated reflection time in your course structure (c).

3. The question "What stands out for you about reflection?" helps spark the reflection process (a).

Chapter 4
Outcome 2: Build Social Connection

> We don't accomplish anything in this world alone . . .
> and whatever happens is the result of the whole tapestry
> of one's life and the weavings of individual threads
> from one to another that creates something.
> —Sandra Day O'Connor, US Supreme Court Justice

Have you ever looked at something for a long time, unable to understand what you are seeing? Maybe you looked at it from different angles, Googled everything you could think of about it, but you were still confused. After working on this book for months, I had that experience when I began struggling with the definitions of *reflection*, *retrieval*, and *metacognition*. The concepts blurred in my mind, leading me to question all the work I'd already poured into these pages.

After a pause to reflect, I asked two people in the L&D book group I host for their advice. I described my dilemma and they shared how they too had found themselves stuck overthinking words and ideas. They helped clarify the terms and gave me the confidence boost I needed to move forward. Clarity, confidence, and camaraderie are just a few of the benefits of social learning.

We often dismiss group learning because we remember less-than-ideal experiences with high school or college group projects. As adults, however, the benefits of learning in groups can be profound:

- **Learning in groups is more efficient than solitary learning, especially when tackling complex tasks.** Working together, we each carry a smaller, more manageable mental load (Kirschner et al. 2009).
- **Reflecting with a group offers unique insights from our peers.** In group-learning situations, we are exposed to a variety of perspectives about the

content. Our colleagues often share surprising views about situations and concepts. My thoughts influence your thoughts, and your thoughts can challenge me to reconsider my perspective.

- **Peers often explain difficult concepts in a more accessible way than facilitators do.** They know our workplace situations firsthand. They can draw relevant analogies and comparisons from shared experiences, making complex concepts easier to understand.
- **The social connections we experience in group-learning situations are invaluable.** These connections improve our motivation to learn, provide emotional support, upgrade our communication skills, and enhance empathy.

I see all these benefits every day in my work. I often hear class participants say breakout rooms are their most valuable experience in training because of the social learning they accomplish as they work through difficult or new concepts.

I agree wholeheartedly with Clark Quinn (2018), who says:

> If we interact with others and hear their interpretations, we'll see different ways of viewing the topic. Having multiple viewpoints is especially important when we're engaged in an activity that requires us to provide a unified output, because we have to negotiate a shared understanding with others. And that enhanced knowledge negotiation enriches each individual's understanding.

Every time we bring people together for training, we need to be aware of the social benefits of learning and how it "enriches each individual's understanding." We must take full advantage of those opportunities. In this chapter, we'll focus on activities that enable social learning while building trust and connection.

Social Connections Enhance the Power of Reflection

I love observing the power of reflection in a group. One person will reveal an idea that then inspires another idea for someone else, which can then lead to a cascade of deeper thinking. Each person brings a unique experience and perspective, pushing discussion and insight past what any one of us can achieve alone. Generally, people with minimal experience in a particular content area benefit the most from collaborative reflection (Renner et al. 2019). That kind of reflection comes in two versions:

- **Veterans helping new learners.** In the Training for Trainers program I run, I regularly watch in awe as seasoned L&D pros support and coach novices with ideas, strategies, and stories of successes and failures. I see the immense relief on people's faces as they discover that they aren't alone in struggling with difficult concepts and that field-tested answers exist for their biggest challenges.
- **New learners helping their peers.** On the other hand, when novice participants work in groups with other inexperienced peers, they tend to feel more secure and face less social pressure around making mistakes. In these settings, new learners show more openness to sharing what they *don't* know, because they're in a group of other beginners who are also willing to ask questions and discuss their mistakes.

A common response I see among new managers in collaborative reflection groups is deep relief when they discover they are not alone. Everyone around them is engaged in similar struggles to provide effective feedback, manage their time, and learn policies they need for success. Suddenly, they are part of a community.

- **Behavior change made easier.** When it comes to the most common goal of any training program—behavior change—reflection combined with social connection is invaluable. The combination helps participants see a variety of new perspectives, and it becomes easier to change behavior. It's difficult to challenge our own thinking if we don't have models to measure ourselves against. When we understand our peers' stories and lived experiences, we gain the measuring stick we need.
- **Start with trust.** Developing trust is the critical first step when integrating social learning into training. Whether your goal is social connection for the sake of improving workplace outcomes or to benefit individual participants, you won't succeed without a foundation of trust among participants. This is why I suggest you always begin with a connection activity to help everyone get comfortable. Rushing into shared reflection without first creating a supportive environment will undermine your efforts.

In the following sections, you will see examples of *pre-flection questions*—for both facilitators and participants—that help build trust. Use these before any of the activities in this chapter to help ensure that your group is ready for social learning.

Questions for Facilitators

There is value in being together and value in shared reflection. Before beginning a reflection activity as a facilitator, ask yourself one or more of these questions:
- Why are these participants together?
- How can they benefit from working together?
- What do you want them to achieve together?

Questions for Participants

Help participants build the trust needed to make supportive social connections. That trust is essential to ensure the activities in this chapter are effective. After presenting some of the information in the training course, but before you begin a reflection activity, ask one or more of the following questions:
- How does this information change how you work together?
- How does this process (or idea) help you move forward?
- How do you feel about how you have worked together so far?
- How could you improve the work you performed?

Activities

Reflection becomes more powerful when done together—whether that's in a classroom, among supportive friends and colleagues, or in a virtual training room. Through shared reflection, we discover we aren't alone in our experiences, doubts, and challenges, which accelerates our learning. The activities that follow are designed to help people connect, share perspectives, and, most important, reflect together.

Learning Maps: Reflections *on* Action, *in* Action

You might be familiar with creating a learning experience map before launching a learning initiative. A learning map is valuable for most people because knowing where you have been and where you are going on a learning journey provides perspective and grounding. In this activity, participants will create a learning map to track their own experiences in real time. The map should highlight topics covered in group discussions and how those topics relate to the workplace. It is a reflection *on* action, *in* action.

Working in small groups provides a level of comfort that encourages people to share their insights and ideas, creating stronger social connections. Small groups also allow easy sharing and comparing of individual maps. When I do this activity, I love discovering what people notice in others' maps that they hadn't considered including in their own. During reflection, everyone has a chance to acknowledge both differences and similarities in their maps.

You'll notice in the following example about learning to make pottery that I include space for my *feelings*, *practice*, and *learning supports*. Those categories represent my efforts to learn and my conflicting emotions. I like the reminder that the learning process is never smooth and rarely predictable.

Katrina's Learning Map: Making Wheel-Thrown Pottery
- Watching *The Great Pottery Throwdown* →
- In-person class →
- Nervous →
- First attempt at the wheel →
- Failed attempt, failed attempt, failed attempt →
- Frustration →
- Watch YouTube videos of *Florian* and *Earth Nation Pottery* →
- In-person class →
- Practice, practice, practice →
- Time away from the wheel for hand building pottery →

Rewatch Season 1 of *The Great Pottery Throwdown*!

While this activity works well for both individuals and small groups, I suggest slightly different approaches for each.

Individual Learning Maps

Ask everyone to create a learning map of their experience in training. Provide an example of your own learning map or use the example I provided. You'll find more examples on my website at katrinakennedy.com/LearningThatLasts.

AT A GLANCE

Reflection Type
- Individual response, private
- Individual response, publicly shared

Delivery Method
- Virtual instructor-led training
- Instructor-led training
- E-learning
- Self-directed learning

Number of Participants
- Any number

Time Needed
- 5–7 minutes

Reflection Time
- During
- After

Step-by-Step Instructions

4. Ask everyone to think about activities that have occurred during the training session.
5. Ask each person to map significant moments and activities on their own large sheet of paper or virtual whiteboard.
6. Encourage them to include emotions, high points, low points, and key support tools (such as job aids, videos, or discussions) and to be creative.
7. Once everyone has finished, invite them to describe their maps to one another in small groups.
8. Debrief with reflection questions:
    - What caught your attention about the maps?
    - What value did creating the map have for you?
    - How does this map help you moving forward?

Facilitator's Guide

What to Say	What to Do
We've done a lot together. We are going to take some time to reflect on everything you've done to reinforce your learning and increase your retention.	
I'd like for you to complete a learning map outlining the activities, accomplishments, thoughts, and feelings you've experienced while learning.	
Here is an example I created.	Show an example learning map.
What are your questions before you get started?	Answer any questions the group has.
Have fun! I'll check in with you as you work.	Monitor the group for questions and clarifications and to gauge time.
Go ahead and wrap up the idea you are on. Thanks for completing your learning maps.	
Optional: Form small groups so you can compare and discuss your learning maps.	Form small groups. Provide prompt questions for the groups: 1. What did you notice? 2. What was hard about the learning map? 3. What was easy about the map? 4. What value did the map have for you? 5. How will you use the map after today?

Small Group Learning Maps

AT A GLANCE

Reflection Type
- Small group response, publicly shared

Delivery Method
- Virtual instructor-led training
- Instructor-led training

Number of Participants
- Groups of 3–5 people

Time Needed
- 10–15 minutes

Reflection Time
- During
- After

Step-by-Step Instructions
1. Form groups of three to five people.
2. Ask everyone to think about activities that have occurred during training.
3. Ask each group to map significant moments and activities on a large sheet of paper or virtual whiteboard.
4. Encourage them to include emotions, high points, low points, and key support tools (such as job aids, videos, or discussions); to be creative; and to include everyone's experiences—even when they differ or contradict one another.
5. Invite each group, once their maps are complete, to describe their maps to the rest of the participants.
6. Debrief with a few reflection questions:
   - What caught your attention or surprised you about the maps?
   - What value did creating the map have for you?
   - How does this map help you moving forward?

Facilitator's Guide

What to Say	What to Do
We've done a lot together. We are going to take some time to reflect on everything you have done to reinforce your learning and increase your retention.	
I'd like you to complete a learning map outlining the activities, accomplishments, thoughts, and feelings you've experienced while learning.	

What to Say	What to Do
Here is an example I created.	Show an example learning map.
We'll form small groups to map your learning experiences together.	Form small groups.
Include everyone's experiences. Be as creative as you'd like.	
What are your questions before you get started?	Answer any questions the groups have.
Have fun! I'll check in with you as you work.	Monitor the groups for questions and clarifications and to gauge time.
Go ahead and wrap up the idea you are on. Thanks for completing your learning maps.	
Let's do a quick debrief together. • What caught your attention about the maps? • What value did creating the map have for you? • How does this map help you moving forward?	

How to Increase the Value
- Post the learning maps in a shared space for everyone to view and add to throughout the training program. Make sharing optional.
- Add pictures, drawings, and emojis to increase visual interest.
- Use Miro or another whiteboard system to make maps digitally viewable.
- Encourage everyone to continue adding to their maps after your time together.

Why I Like This Activity
When I create my own learning maps, they help me reflect on my journey, reminding me of the ups and downs I've endured. When participants in training programs that I facilitate create learning maps, I appreciate seeing their progress.

When any of us revisits difficult moments through reflection, we can sometimes recall intricate details or processes that we might otherwise forget and that are valuable in the learning process. For example, when reflecting on my pottery learning map, I'd initially overlooked my first class attempt as I focused on the second difficult class.

This activity can also work well for outcome 8, self-awareness.

Give It a Try

Consider something you've learned recently. Map out your process. Consider highs and lows, your feelings, learning support, and any other critical experiences.

My Learning Map

NOW ASK YOURSELF

- When could you use a learning map?
- For which of the groups you train would this reflection work well?
- How could you alter this activity to fit a program you are designing?
- What tools or resources are available to you for creating a learning map?

Shared Learning Map

Group size is the primary difference between the previous activity and this one. The shared learning map is a larger group experience, while the learning map can be an individual or small-group experience.

To create a shared learning map, all participants work together. After individually reflecting on their experiences, everyone contributes their reflections to one grand paper, whiteboard, or virtual whiteboard map. This common reference point helps all participants fill in gaps, see connections, and benefit from one another's perspectives. Naturally, creating a large group map will take more time than creating a small group map.

A shared learning map provides participants and facilitators with a fabulous visual representation of their time together. When highs and lows are mapped, everyone gains new insights along the way and a true sense of the training experience as a whole. After one group created a shared map for a multi-day program I facilitated, one person expressed her disbelief at everything the class had learned together—something that would not have been as apparent without the visual representation (Figure 4-1).

Figure 4-1. A Shared Learning Map: Emerging Leaders Program

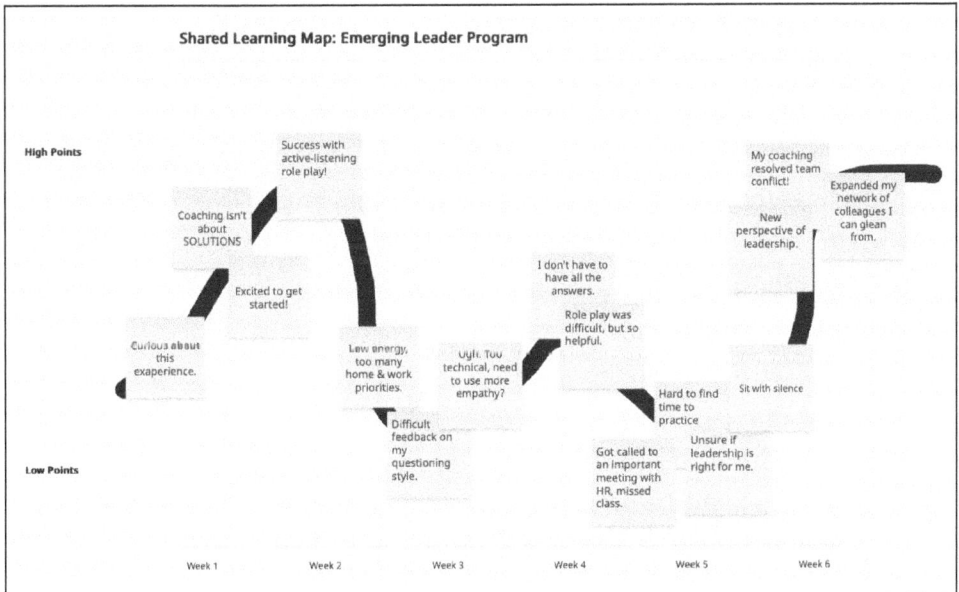

While this activity works well for both virtual and in-person training, I suggest slightly different approaches for each.

AT A GLANCE	
Reflection Type • Large group response	**Number of Participants** • 2 to unlimited
Delivery Method • Virtual instructor-led training • Instructor-led training • E-learning	**Time** • 15–20 minutes **Reflection Timing** • During • After

The Virtual Instructor-Led Training (vILT) Activity

Provide a shared virtual whiteboard or blank slide for participants to use as the base of their map. Invite everyone to first consider high points and key insights from the training course. Ask them to place their experiences, feelings, moments, high points, and low points on the map. Don't worry about duplicate information or differing perspectives. When they're done, ask members of the group to discuss what they notice as most significant or surprising in the final version and clarify anything they don't understand.

Step-by-Step Instructions

1. Ask everyone to think about the activities that have occurred during training.
2. Ask them to map the activities on a virtual whiteboard.
3. Encourage participants to include high and low points, key ideas, insights, and feelings they've experienced. The map should mirror lived experience.
4. When the map appears complete, conduct a debrief. Consider these questions:
    - What stands out for you?
    - What did you like about this process?
    - What was difficult about this process?
    - What did you learn as you completed the shared learning map?
    - What effect will the learning map have on your work?

Facilitator's Guide

What to Say	What to Do
Let's take time to consider everything we've experienced together.	
We're going to create a map to show the journey we've been on. It can include your highs and lows, victories, and failures. Share your feelings and anything else that represents your experience.	
Here is an example to get us started.	Show a shared learning map example.
When you are ready, begin to add your experiences to the board. Add as many as you'd like. Don't worry about duplicates or differing experiences.	Provide any clarification needed. Monitor time.
Please wrap up your last idea.	
Look at the work you've done. What stands out for you?	Hold a debrief discussion about the shared learning map experience.

The Instructor-Led Training (ILT) Activity

Place a large whiteboard or multiple chart pages on a wall, and invite everyone to consider their high points and key insights from the training course. Ask them to place their experiences, feelings, important moments, high points, and low points on the map. Use sticky notes to readjust the map as it's created. Don't worry about duplicate information or differing perspectives. When they're done, ask everyone to step back and discuss what they notice as most significant or surprising in the final version, and clarify anything they don't understand.

Step-by-Step Instructions

1. Ask everyone to think about activities that have occurred during training.
2. Ask them to map the activities to a large whiteboard or multiple chart pages posted on the wall.
3. Encourage them to include high and low points, key ideas, insights, and feelings they've experienced. The map should mirror their lived experience.
4. Encourage everyone to discuss ideas and concepts as they put them in writing.

5. When the map appears to be complete, conduct a debrief. Consider these questions:
   - What stands out for you?
   - What did you like about this process?
   - What did you dislike about this process?
   - What did you learn as you completed the shared learning map?
   - What effect will the learning map have on your work?

Facilitator's Guide

What to Say	What to Do
Let's take time to consider everything we've experienced together.	
We're going to create a map to show the journey we've been on. It can include your highs and lows, victories, and failures. Share your feelings and anything else that represents your experience.	
Here is an example to get us started.	Show a shared learning map example.
When you are ready, begin to add your experiences to the board. Add as many as you'd like. Don't worry about duplicates or differing experiences.	Provide any clarification needed. Monitor time.
Please wrap up your last idea.	
Look at the work you've done. What stands out for you?	Hold a debrief discussion about the shared learning map experience.

How to Increase the Value

- Start the map at the beginning of class. Invite people to add high points and insights throughout class. At key points, pause occasionally to ask people to reflect.
- Use a Miro or Zoom whiteboard to create a virtual learning map for reference and follow up after the program is complete.
- Instead of a simple map, try creating a reflection tree. Oyindamola Ojo-Eriamiatoe, director of Beccamola and founder of eLearning and Instructional Designers Hub, created a beautiful version of this variation on a learning map. Each branch of the tree represented a portion of a multiple-part session, onto which participants added colorful sticky notes with their takeaways.

Why I Like This Activity

Whenever I do this activity, I look forward to seeing the learning maps come together. Each map acknowledges individual experiences while also revealing the collective experience. The shared maps I love most are those that inspire participants to take selfies with their work.

Making our thinking more visual can help us all create a shared experience, and visuals can also help us, as trainers and designers, see the results of what we've worked to convey.

NOW ASK YOURSELF

- When could you use a shared learning map?
- Which groups would this reflection activity work well for?
- How could you alter this activity to fit your training programs?
- What would inspire people to take selfies with their work in your organization?

I Would Title This . . .

We all like naming things—our sports teams, our pets, and even our cars. Why not name our learning experiences as well? In this activity, you'll ask participants to think about a complete training course and sum it up in one phrase. This is usually a fun and thought-provoking reflection activity. It's a creative way to appeal to your participants' feelings and intellect at the same time.

In the following example, I've asked for a movie title, but consider your participants and choose a category that works well for them. You might ask for the title of a movie, book, video game, breakfast cereal, or something else that's especially appealing to the participants.

AT A GLANCE

Reflection Type
- Individual response, publicly shared
- Small group response, publicly shared

Delivery Method
- Virtual instructor-led training
- Instructor-led training

Number of Participants
- Any number

Time Needed
- 7–10 minutes

Reflection Timing
- Before

The Activity

You'll ask everyone to pause and consider a completed learning experience. Then, ask them to think of a title that would fit their experience. They can borrow from a book, movie, or song. They might create a fun riff on an existing title or make up an original one. Puns and wordplay are encouraged!

Step-by-Step Instructions

1. Ask everyone to consider their entire experience together and sum it up with an appropriate movie, book, or song title.
2. Provide an example and enough time (seven to 10 minutes) for a little creative reflection to occur.
3. Ask individuals or groups to write down their titles.
4. Ask individuals or groups to share their titles.
5. Ask everyone to discuss the value of the reflection.

Facilitator's Guide

What to Say	What to Do
Let's look back on our entire experience together.	
If you were to give it a movie title, what would you call it?	
Here's my example.	Show a slide of your example.
I'll give you a few minutes to consider your title. When you are ready, add your title to our whiteboard.	Pause for everyone to think and write their titles.
Do you want to know the motivation behind any of the titles? If so, which ones?	Give everyone an opportunity to ask about specific titles, inviting the title owner to share their motivation.

How to Increase the Value

- Ask groups to create a visual representation of their title to display in your room or virtual space.
- Conclude with a few quick reflection questions, such as:
  - What themes do you see running through all the titles?
  - What did you learn from creating titles together?
- Use a virtual tool like Padlet to collect everyone's titles.

Why I Like This Activity

This activity requires more patience than I typically have! Although I initially worry it's too challenging, because participants often take a minute or two to warm to it, I've learned that the pause serves an important purpose. Those quiet moments give everyone time to both reflect on their shared experience and prepare to think creatively.

The creativity that flows from participants always catches me by surprise, makes me laugh, or excites me. For example, in a training program on creative use of PowerPoint, one participant shared "Mighty Morphin' PowerPoint Rangers" as his title, making the entire class chuckle. Morph happens to be a fun PowerPoint transition people love learning to use.

Give It a Try

Think of what you've read about so far in this book or another book you've read recently. Give it a title (other than the obvious title on the cover!) and write it down in the space provided.

I Would Title This . . .

NOW ASK YOURSELF

- When could you use this activity?
- Which groups would this reflection work well for?
- How could you alter this activity to fit your training program?
- What will you use? Breakfast cereals, movies, books, or other common interests?

Draw a Mind Map

Do you find flowcharts helpful? A mind map is a flowchart mapping our thought process and a classic method of collecting and sorting ideas. When we make our ideas visual in this way, we increase the benefits of social reflection because we create a shared view of our experience. We also reveal more about our differences of opinion and perspective.

We begin a mind map by retrieving the concepts covered in training. The map becomes a powerful reflection tool as participants each add more thoughts and feelings. Participants' mind maps can begin with a central theme or outcome and then expand with branches stretching out to show supporting ideas. Mind maps work well in both digital and analog formats. In Figure 4-2, you'll see an example of a mind map I created to show my writing process.

Figure 4-2. Katrina's Writing Process Mapped

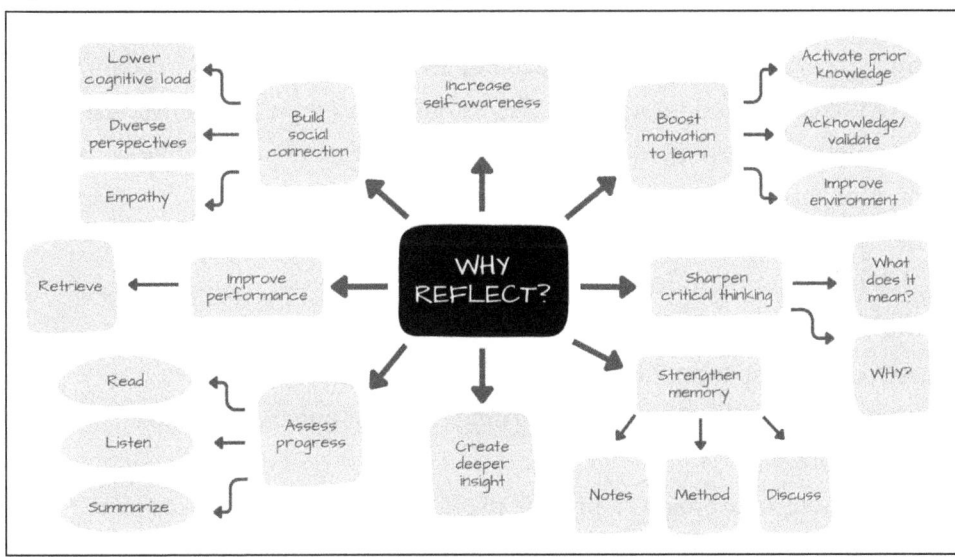

AT A GLANCE

Reflection Type
- Individual response, private
- Individual response, publicly shared
- Small group response, publicly shared
- Large group response

Delivery Method
- Virtual instructor-led training
- Instructor-led training
- E-learning
- Self-directed learning

Number of Participants
- Any number

Time Needed
- 5–10 minutes

Reflection Timing
- During
- After

The Activity

Provide everyone with a mind map template, either digital or in a paper handout. It can be as simple as a box in the middle they draw lines from or more complex like Figure 4-2. Adjust the style of the mind map to fit the group. Show them an example from another class or project and invite each participant to begin with a topic in the center and then create arrows outward for each objective. Ask them to write all they can recall for each objective. Encourage sharing activities, experiences, thoughts, and feelings.

Step-by-Step Instructions

1. Introduce the mind map concept.
2. Provide participants with a basic mind map with a few branches labeled to correspond with key learning points or outcomes related to your program.
3. Throughout your program, provide two-to-three-minute pauses to give everyone time to reflect on what has been covered and add it to their mind maps.
4. Ask participants to share and compare with others if they're comfortable doing so.
5. At the end of your program, provide an opportunity for everyone to share and discuss highlights of their mind maps.
6. Encourage everyone to reference and continue to add to their maps when they return to work.

Facilitator's Guide

What to Say	What to Do
We are going to use a mind map to reflect on what we've experienced together.	
Think of all the things we've done together, as well as anything you've learned along the way.	
I'll place our topic in the center. Each branch represents our learning objectives.	Put the topic in the center.
Now, it's your turn to add to the map. Branch as much as you'd like, adding as much detail as you'd like.	Monitor time and provide any clarification needed.
Take a step back and look at what you've created.	
Optional: Let's do a quick debrief of your process. • What stands out for you? • How did it feel to create the mind map? • What value did creating the mind map have for you? • What actions does this mind map trigger for you?	

How to Increase the Value

- Consider creating individual, small group, and large group mind maps.
- Send a link to your own interactive mind map to everyone in the class. Ask them to add any actions or ideas they've gathered since they created the map.
- Use a tool like Miro or Mural to create a virtual mind map.

Why I Like This Activity

I often ask groups to create a virtual mind map at the end of class. I put the course goal in the center with a branch for each objective. I then ask everyone to draw everything they can recall. I'm always amazed at the result. People often create new branches with small details of importance to specific participants.

Figures 4-3 and 4-4 are examples of mind maps from two different groups reflecting on the same training analysis. They were given the four main branches, but the remaining text and annotations were added by participants.

Figure 4-3. Mind Map 1

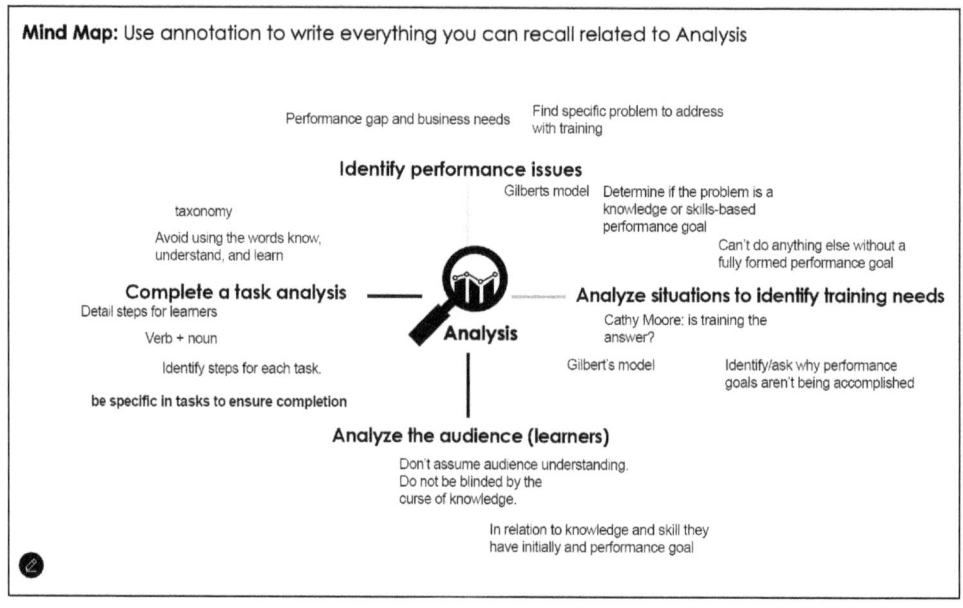

Figure 4-4. Mind Map 2

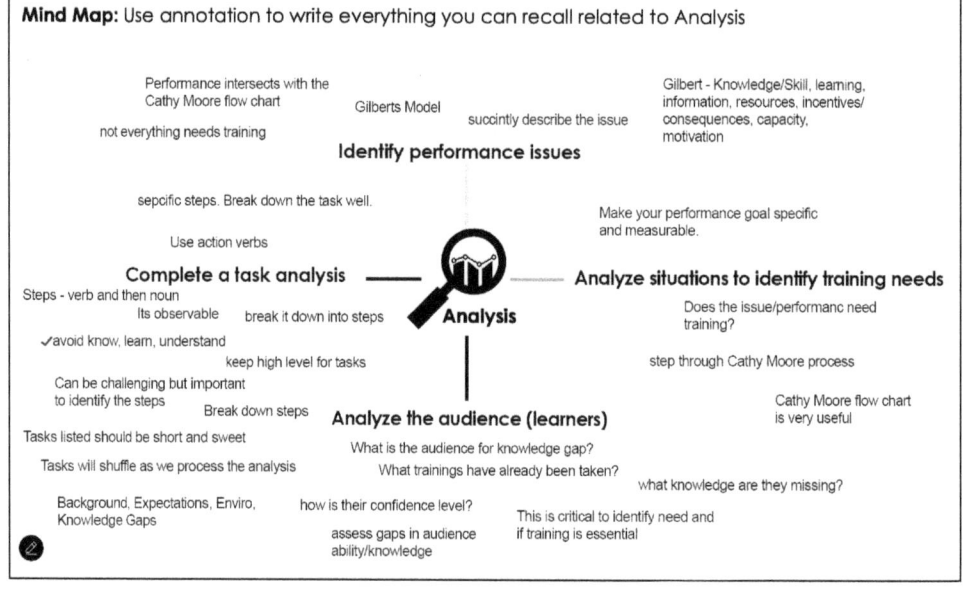

Give It a Try

In the space provided, draw your own mind map, starting with the figure in the middle. Use your thoughts about this chapter or the most recent training course you've been a part of as your starting point.

My Mind Map

NOW ASK YOURSELF

- When could you use the Draw a Mind Map activity?
- Which groups would this reflection work well for?
- How could you alter this activity to fit training you are designing?

Reflect, Pair, Share

This is my take on the classic learning strategy Think, Pair, Share. Reflect, Pair, Share works well for reflection both in person and during virtual learning experiences. It allows participants to combine individual reflection with the benefits of paired reflection. Paired reflection is valuable because it's been shown to increase engagement and retention and lead to better performance outcomes. In other words, we are stronger together!

AT A GLANCE

Reflection Type
- Individual response, publicly shared
- Paired response, private
- Paired response, publicly shared
- Small group response, private
- Small group response, publicly shared

Delivery Method
- Virtual instructor-led training
- Instructor-led training

Number of Participants
- Any number

Time Needed
- 10–15 minutes

Reflection Timing
- During
- After

The Activity

You will ask each participant to reflect individually on their learning experience with a set of reflection questions. Once they've completed their individual reflections, they will connect in pairs to share their reflections. Their discussion provides an opportunity to confirm their reflections and a chance to expand their perspective by exploring their partner's reflection.

Step-by-Step Instructions

1. Provide a question for participants to consider individually. Some examples include:
   - What went well for you today?
   - What did you learn from this experience, class, or activity?
   - What was the value of this experience, class, or activity?
   - How will you implement what you've learned in your own work?
   - What was difficult for you? What was easy?
2. Ask everyone to form pairs and share their reflections, encouraging them to share only what they are comfortable with.
3. Debrief as a larger group. (This is recommended, but not required.)

Facilitator's Guide

What to Say	What to Do
We are going to take a moment to reflect on your experience. Reflection will help you retain information and transfer your experiences to the work you do.	
Here is a question I'd like you to reflect on for a couple minutes.	Show the question and monitor time.
Great. Now please connect in pairs and share your reflections on the question as much as you're comfortable with. You'll have about 10 minutes.	Monitor time and stay available for questions.
Thank you for sharing! Let's come back together now.	
Optional: Would anyone like to share some of what you discussed with the larger group?	

How to Increase the Value

- Invite pairs of participants to share their reflections repeatedly through a longer program. This can encourage relationship building and deeper reflection.
- Encourage ongoing sharing after the formal program has ended. Create accountability partners or reflection buddies.

Why I Like This Activity

Think, Pair, Share is a classic tool for educators and trainers because it works so well. Repurposing the tool for reflection just makes sense.

Participants feel safer sharing in pairs and small groups. Even reluctant participants find comfort in the initial step of thinking alone because it helps them prepare what they're going to say when they reach the sharing step.

I've seen many quiet participants transform when given the opportunity to first think alone and then share in a pair with no obligation to report to the entire group. It's one more way to create inclusive learning that lasts.

Worried about uneven groups? A group of three works just as well.

Give It a Try

In the space provided, reflect on the questions asked. Then, find someone you can share your reflection with. Do you want to find someone who is reading this book? Pop on over to LinkedIn (linkedin.com/in/KatrinaKennedyTraining) and I'll help connect you with someone.

Reflect, Pair, Share

1. What have you found valuable about reflection so far?

2. How can you use the reflection activities in your future work?

3. What challenges do you anticipate in adding reflection activities to training?

NOW ASK YOURSELF

- When could you use Reflect, Pair, Share?
- Which groups would this reflection work well for?
- How could you alter this activity to fit your training program?

Conclusion

We all remember frustrating group projects in high school or college, usually completed by one or two dedicated classmates while others avoided doing anything at all. But in workplace training focused on reflection, our group work experiences can and should have far more value and more productive results. With a little structure and some well-crafted questions, participants can experience successful reflection in pairs and both small and large groups.

The ideal result: The participants form powerful, effective, and sometimes long-lasting social connections.

Why are group reflection activities so effective? Simply put, what you know helps increase what I know and what the larger group knows. Together, we can solve more complex problems, identify hidden perspectives, and create options we wouldn't consider alone.

In this chapter, you explored activities to increase social connection:

1. **Learning Map:** A visual map created to track the learning experience of individuals and small groups
2. **Shared Learning Map:** A large, crowdsourced map documenting the learning journeys of everyone involved in a learning experience
3. **I Would Title This . . .:** A lighthearted approach to reflection that labels a learning experience with a related title, helping people consider their experience in a creative way
4. **Draw a Mind Map:** A map of key elements participants can recall from a course, along with the actions they'll take after training
5. **Reflect, Pair, Share:** A twist on a classic activity focused on identifying key actions to take in the workplace

We know that the social connections created through group reflection often benefit participants as much as sharing content knowledge. Social connections help improve employee well-being, learning, and productivity. For this reason, I usually suggest that learning experiences begin with individual reflection and then almost always move on to group reflection.

Keep in mind that social connection activities like those in this chapter are most useful when the learning objectives require collaboration, cooperation, and problem solving. Participants in the activities can build on initial learning through reflection and support one another, reflecting what they hope to achieve later in the workplace.

FINAL QUESTIONS FOR REFLECTION

To increase social connection, consider including these questions when completing any group-learning activity:

- What did we accomplish together?
- How did you benefit from your group's input?
- What was the value of working together?
- What do you need from the group?

Chapter 5
Outcome 3: Strengthen Memory

> We do not learn from experience.
> We learn from reflecting on experience.
> —John Dewey, philosopher, psychologist, and education reformer

Which of these math problems can you answer?
- $2 \times 2 =$
- $4 \times 4 =$
- $10 \times 10 =$

Chances are you can complete all these equations quickly, without much thought. Do you *need* to know them, though? You probably have devices within easy reach that can show you the answers accurately and quickly, with little effort required. However, in our daily lives, being able to do some basic math without hesitation often allows us to save time and maneuver through other difficult concepts. The same is true if we can quickly recall policies, procedures, and other skills and knowledge. Despite all the technology we have available, committing some information to memory is still worthwhile.

As L&D professionals, we often ask ourselves what people *really* need to remember to do their jobs effectively and efficiently. Most employees must commit to memory at least some elements of their jobs. Surgeons, pilots, and nuclear power plant operators use lengthy checklists to complete complex tasks, but they also call upon details memorized from their academic and on-the-job training to complete routine tasks and successfully navigate tense emergency situations.

Consider the most recent training course you developed or facilitated. Was there information you needed everyone to quickly remember, without consulting the internet, job aids, or other references?

Working from memory can increase speed and accuracy and reduce the cognitive load required during complex tasks, so time invested in memorizing critical information is well spent (Kurdi et al. 2018). In this chapter, we'll talk about how pausing for reflection improves memory.

Reflection Leads to Retention

In my first job after college, I was a family support officer. I had to determine the amount of child support that noncustodial parents were responsible for paying. I applied a complex formula accounting for the person's income, a limited number of their expenses, and their percentage of court-determined custody, using a calculator, a pen, and paper. To calculate the amount precisely, I often conducted an in-person interview with the noncustodial parent. I referenced several checklists and a massive physical manual to determine the amount. These were cumbersome to haul around and embarrassing to use in front of nervous or angry parents.

It did not take long for me to realize that committing some information to memory was essential and could free me from some of the burden of my paper references. I now know that reflection activities, including some of those described in this chapter, could have made my learning faster and more durable. I probably would have made fewer mistakes as well.

Pay Attention and Learn

Attention, retrieval, reflection, and learning work together in an interconnected process. Paying attention strengthens our ability to encode new information, the crucial first step in storing memories. Retrieving information strengthens its place in our long-term memory. Reflecting on retrieved information helps us uncover its value and identify actionable insights.

You are probably aware of many moments in the past year when you've started to drift off during meetings, training, or conversations. Adding reflection activities throughout training and meetings can help minimize mental wandering by emphasizing the relevance of content we are covering.

If we've grabbed a participant's attention, we are preparing them for learning and remembering. Reflection after important objectives helps participants store ideas in long-term memory by allowing them to consider what they learned, connect it to their work, and increase the likelihood that they'll retain it.

Before you move forward in the next training program you design or deliver, take a moment to reflect on what you want people to remember. This will help you choose the activities that work best for your participants.

Questions for Instructional Designers and Facilitators

Think of a learning experience you anticipate designing or delivering soon.
- What do participants need to remember to perform their jobs?
- What areas are supported by checklists and job aids?
- How will you include reflection to support memory formation?

A MEMORY STRENGTHENER

When designing activities to strengthen memory, consider using both brief and more in-depth reflection activities. Add quick reflection questions throughout the program. And then include longer, more comprehensive reflection exercises like those in this chapter at key points.

Quick reflection questions to help strengthen memory might include:

- What does this information mean?
- What words or phrases stood out for you?
- Can you rephrase this in your own words?
- What does this information mean?
- How could you apply this in your own work?

Activities

This chapter's activities will help people reflect on their learning experiences and strengthen their memory. Strengthening memory is about time—taking time to thoughtfully reflect on what is being experienced as well as the value and meaning of those experiences.

Often, intentional reflection time can be more powerful than more practice when it comes to improving memory. Remember, although we've all been told that practice makes perfect, the phrase should be, *practice and reflection move us closer to perfect performance!*

Five Bullet Points

If I gave you the choice of recalling 12 things or five things, which option would you select? Most of us would opt for five because it's a more manageable number. A little more thought is required to recall five things than three, but remembering five things is still easier than remembering 12.

The Five Bullet Points activity challenges participants to reflect on an activity or a piece of content by creating a list of five actions or insights. Five is not a random number. Most of us can hold five items in our short-term memory, although this isn't a universal rule. Some researchers suggest that we keep fewer than five chunks of information in our short-term memory and that the size of our chunks differ (Doumont 2002).

AT A GLANCE

Reflection Type
- Individual response, private
- Individual response, publicly shared
- Small group response, publicly shared

Delivery Method
- Virtual instructor-led training
- Instructor-led training
- E-learning
- Self-directed learning

Number of Participants
- Any number

Time Needed
- 5–7 minutes

Reflection Timing
- During
- After

The Activity

You will select a reflection focus. Let participants know that they will be asked to reflect on their experiences and identify five responses to a focus prompt.

Reflection focus prompts might include:
- Identify five actions you are going to take.
- Identify five ways to practice what you've learned.
- Identify five obstacles to implementing the ideas discussed in class.
- Identify five things you've learned today.
- Identify five ways you were surprised by the content.

You'll then ask everyone to brainstorm individually before asking a few people to share one or two of their bullet points with the group. Alternatively, you may ask participants to form small groups to create lists of five items.

Step-by-Step Instructions for Individuals
1. Select the reflection focus for the group.
2. Ask each person to individually brainstorm their five responses to the prompt.
3. When everyone is done, ask people to share one or two of their bullet points.

Step-by-Step Instructions for Small Groups
1. Form small groups of three to five people.
2. Ask each small group to brainstorm responses to the prompt.
3. Ask each small group to create a list of five responses.
4. Invite a representative from each group to share one or two bullet points from their list.

Facilitator's Guide

What to Say	What to Do
We're going to take a moment to identify five ideas from class.	
Take a moment to consider five actions you are going to take after class.	Display the prompt. Adjust it for your content and purpose.
Write down your five actions.	Monitor time and provide clarification if needed.
Thank you for taking the time to reflect on your actions. I'd love to hear a few of the actions you are going to take.	Acknowledge several participants' actions.

How to Increase the Value
- Use this activity at the beginning of a program to ask participants to identify five things they want to accomplish. Return to it at the end so they can analyze their list and add five more bullet points for implementation.
- Ask individuals to write down their five bullet points. Then, form groups to create a collaborative list of five items that everyone in the group agrees on.

Why I Like This Activity
Writing and talking about our five items will help us recall them later. I'm often pleasantly surprised by what people add to their lists. They sometimes contain phrases used in class, as well as their individual insights.

I love that there is no wrong way to go about completing this activity.

Give It a Try

Consider what you've read about reflection for learning, either today or in the past. Identify five insights about the topic in the space provided.

These are my five insights about reflection for learning:

1. _____

2. _____

3. _____

4. _____

5. _____

Now, change the prompt's focus to action to create a different reflective perspective.

Identify five actions you can take to enhance your work as an L&D professional after learning more about reflection:

1. I will _____

2. I will _____

3. I will _____

4. I will _____

5. I will _____

NOW ASK YOURSELF

- When could you use Five Bullet Points?
- Which participants would this reflection work well for?
- How could you alter this activity to fit the training courses you design or deliver?
- What reflection focus will you use?

One Question

How many questions do you ask in a typical class? We all spend a substantial amount of time asking participants questions, but what if we flipped the concept? Instead of asking people to answer our questions, we would ask them to write their own questions, which they would then use to reflect on the topic.

The value of this activity is that participants are given time to think through a variety of questions that go beyond those that first come to mind. Reflection happens both when writing the questions and when considering the answers. This can lead to discovering new perspectives that participants haven't considered.

While they may share their questions with the facilitator or with their peers, sharing isn't a required part of this activity. The power and learning happen as a result of formulating the questions.

AT A GLANCE

Reflection Type
- Individual response, publicly shared

Delivery Method
- Virtual instructor-led training
- Instructor-led training

Number of Participants
- 1–20
- This activity works best with small groups

Time Needed
- 2 minutes for individual reflection
- 10 minutes for group discussion
- For multisession experiences, consider repeating the activity each session

Reflection Timing
- During
- After

The Activity

In this activity, everyone writes a question they have about the content or activity you've completed as a group. Write on a 3x5 card or sticky note; if learning virtually, use a virtual whiteboard or survey app such as Slido or Mentimeter.

You'll pause for question writing and stop periodically, asking everyone to consider all the questions they've written. Provide additional time for participants to consider how they might answer the questions. Consider inviting everyone to write their responses.

Questions can be anonymous or discussed in small groups. Both variations have advantages. The point of this activity is not for the facilitator to answer all the questions but to encourage everyone to explore the questions that come to mind for them.

Step-by-Step Instructions
1. Give everyone sticky notes or 3x5 cards.
   - Alternatively, ask them to use a handout or digital document to record their questions.
2. Encourage participants to write any questions on the notes as you move through class together.
3. Pause from time to time to invite everyone to record their questions.
4. Pause at some point to ask everyone to choose a question to reflect on.
5. Provide time for reflection.
6. Repeat the process as time allows.
7. Toward the conclusion of your program, ask everyone to grab one question they've written. Give them time (two to five minutes) to formulate responses.
8. Encourage participants to place any questions they can't answer in a designated location.
9. Ask everyone to answer any questions they can.

Facilitator's Guide

What to Say	What to Do
We're going to set up a reflection activity that we'll use throughout training.	
I'll pause from time to time and ask you to think of one question you have about the content or activity. It can be a question you know the answer to or something you are just wondering. I'll invite you to share your questions, but it's not required. The value of this activity is in considering and reflecting on the questions.	Provide sticky notes or 3x5 cards.
Take a moment now and write your question. Keep it somewhere you can find later.	Alternatively, share a space where questions can be posted.

What to Say	What to Do
	Let some time go by.
Let's look at your questions. Who would like to share one they wrote?	Lead a discussion about the question. Prompt the group. Provide your insight only when the group obviously has nothing more to add.
	Repeat question writing and discussion throughout the program.

How to Increase the Value
- Add additional time for participants to reflect on their questions after they've been discussed. Additional reflection will help participants process the new information and retain insight.
- Form pairs of participants to discuss the questions they've written. This provides perspective, and an opportunity to reflect on one another's questions. The additional conversation can help strengthen memory.
- Ask everyone to post their questions in a shared space. Invite them to remove their questions or move them to a new location when they have been answered.
- Invite people to hand you any urgent questions they'd like to have answered, keeping a stack of questions to answer as time permits.

Why I Like This Activity
Can one question really have a big influence on learning?

I've discovered that when we are forced to consider our own questions, we often realize that we know more than we thought. The questions we ask reveal what we are struggling with. Thinking about what we are uncertain of can prompt deeper thinking and reveal ideas we had not considered. We also feel validated when we discover that our peers have similar questions.

I love collecting participants' stacks of 3x5 cards or sticky notes full of questions, especially those questions they find difficult to answer. I try to provide insight and answers, or I reference them as I design future programs.

Give It a Try

Consider the following question and respond in the space provided. Your responses can be simple or complex. You can write one or many. You decide.

What questions do you have about strengthening memory?

NOW ASK YOURSELF

- When could you use the One Question activity?
- Which participants would this reflection work well for?
- How could you alter this activity to fit your training program?

The Spinning Wheel of Wonder

Novelty in training boosts engagement and provides a fun opportunity for group reflection and a little laughter. The Spinning Wheel of Wonder (Figure 5-1) is a novel approach and a crowd favorite. However, it's not novelty for novelty's sake. The Spinning Wheel of Wonder is a low-tech, highly engaging method to reflect on learning as a group.

Figure 5-1. The Spinning Wheel of Wonder

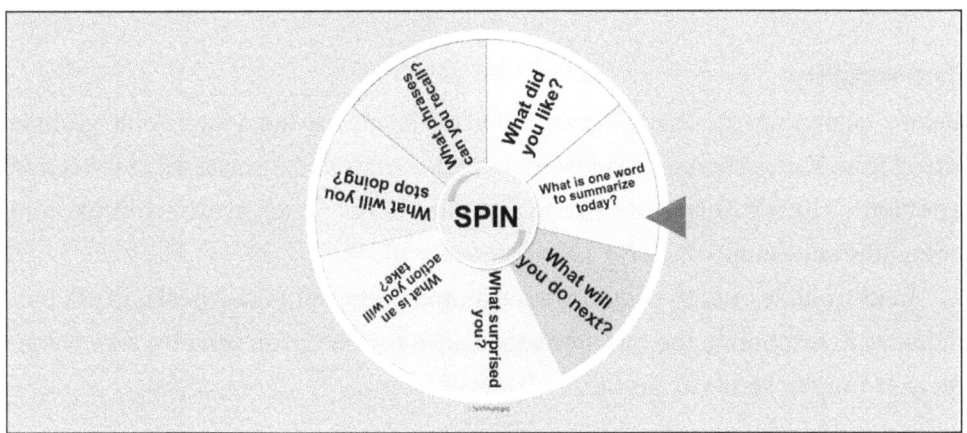

For this activity, a participant spins a digital wheel to reveal a question. The group can answer spontaneously, or you can call on people (as long as you warn them beforehand, and this works for your group). You can also take a volunteer who then volunteers someone else. You have choices!

The last time I used the Spinning Wheel of Wonder, I used the popcorn technique—in which one person picks the next person—because the group was small, and people were comfortable with one another. I have also shared the wheel to Zoom breakout rooms, and in that case, I spin, and they discuss the question in smaller groups.

> **CONSIDER YOUR PARTICIPANTS**
>
> The Spinning Wheel of Wonder is novel and fun for some people. But it can also be distracting and dizzying for some participants. Provide a warning like the one in the Facilitator's Guide for those who may want to look away or opt out.
>
> If you are presenting virtually, participants may experience some lag in video or audio if connections aren't strong. If that's the case, add a few extra seconds to allow for asking and answering questions.

AT A GLANCE

Reflection Type
- Large group response

Delivery Method
- Virtual instructor-led training
- Instructor-led training

Number of Participants
- 2–24

Time Needed
- 5–10 minutes

Reflection Timing
- During
- After

The Activity

Before beginning the learning experience, download the PowerPoint graphic wheel from KatrinaKennedy.com/LearningThatLasts and insert a set of reflection questions. Alternatively, you can use an online service such as wheeldecide.com or spinthewheel.app.

In the middle or at the end of your training event, spin the wheel and ask participants to respond to the question aloud or in the chat. You can also take volunteers or work in teams to answer.

Step-by-Step Instructions

1. Add a set of reflection questions to your wheel of choice. Those questions can include:
   - What phrases can you recall?
   - What did you like?
   - What is one word to summarize today?
   - What will you do next?
   - What surprised you?
   - What is something you will do immediately?
   - What is something you'll stop doing?
2. At the midpoint or end of your program, let everyone know you are going to use the Spinning Wheel of Wonder!
3. Display the wheel.
4. Briefly explain how it works. Mention that the activity involves some visual motion that some participants may find uncomfortable. Let people know they can look away if they're sensitive to moving images.
5. Ask for a volunteer to answer the first question or tell participants to shout out answers.

6. Spin the wheel, encouraging the volunteer or group to tell you when to stop.
7. When the wheel stops, read the question.
8. After the first volunteer responds, ask them to pick the next person (or take shouted answers from the group).
9. Repeat the process until your allotted time is complete.

Facilitator's Guide

What to Say	What to Do
Ready for the Spinning Wheel of Wonder?	Show the PowerPoint slide with the Spinning Wheel of Wonder.
We are going to use the Spinning Wheel of Wonder to reflect on your class experience. I'll spin the wheel, and you tell me when to stop. Once I stop, I'll ask the question. You can shout out the answer or put it into the chat.	
The Spinning Wheel of Wonder contains motion that may cause discomfort for some viewers. If you're sensitive to moving images, you may wish to look away or step out briefly.	
Ready?	Spin the wheel. Read the question that the wheel lands on. Wait for responses before spinning the wheel again.
	Repeat until your allotted time is complete.

How to Increase the Value

- Ask everyone to write questions to include on the Spinning Wheel of Wonder throughout your training course. Keep them short and precise. Then, use the wheel as a tool for final reflections.
- Share the Spinning Wheel of Wonder to virtual breakout groups. Spin the wheel. Ask groups to answer and discuss each question as it appears. Spin the wheel, allow two minutes for discussion, and then spin it again.

Why I Like This Activity

In my experience, people love the Spinning Wheel of Wonder! It appeals to our memories of TV game shows or game nights with friends and family.

The more questions I include, the more random the spin becomes and the better everyone's experience is. I like to include serious reflective questions along with a few fun questions that allow people to share their opinions. Questions like "What is something funny you recall from class?" and "Who has helped you during class?" are crowd favorites.

Everyone benefits from the reflection questions, whether they respond or just listen.

Give It a Try

Spin the sample Spinning Wheel of Wonder that I've uploaded on my website (katrinakennedy.com/LearningThatLasts) and answer the reflection question in the space provided.

NOW ASK YOURSELF

- When could you use the Spinning Wheel of Wonder?
- Which participants would this reflection activity work well for?
- How could you alter the Spinning Wheel of Wonder for programs you design or deliver?
- What questions will you include on your Spinning Wheel?

Fill In Your Box

Do you have virtual participants who don't engage? Building accountability and a little peer pressure into learning can entice people into participating when they might otherwise sit back and quietly observe.

Fill In Your Box invites everyone to add a sentence or a comment to their box on a PowerPoint slide deck or whiteboard. Seeing their name on the screen with an empty space to fill can prompt engagement and reflection. Everyone also sees high points from their peers, further enhancing reflection.

You can see in this Fill In Your Box class example (Figure 5-2) that some people share a lot, while others just provide brief reflections. Once squares fill in, I invite everyone to stamp ideas that resonated with them. I love to watch the screen fill with hearts and stars.

Figure 5-2. Fill In Your Box

Suresh More often, the environmental factors influence the performance. The individual factors are usually secondary. Training only resolves one factor affecting performance. Wholistic approach looks into all 6 factors and approach solution accordingly.	John Start with environmental influence before individual when considering issues	Talisen Train for knowledge
Katy Metacognition	Kaitlin ADDIE, Gilbert's model (assessment of need starts with environment and goes from there).	Trina training is performance based and learner focused trainings are good for knowledge/skills related performance issues analyze, design, develop, implement, and evaluate there are five stages for training projects
Chris Jumping in to join a great discussion about analyzing the reason for performance issues	Davy Not all performance issues can be solved with training	Jessica Our working memory can hold 3-5 items at a time.
Elizabeth You must have interaction and engagement in trainings for them to be effective. The most important thing is engagement rather than just dumpint all of the information on them. The way they will learn is through engagement and interaction instead of just having all the info dumped on them.	Michelle Information vs knowledge ♥ John's whole team is here!	Katrina Elizabeth's question about invormation vs. knowledge Suresh's question about guessing on Pretest No one recalled metacognition

AT A GLANCE

Reflection Type
- Individual response, publicly shared

Delivery Method
- Virtual instructor-led training

Number of Participants
- 2–24

Time Needed
- 6–8 minutes

Reflection Timing
- During
- After

The Activity

At a reflection point, display a PowerPoint grid on your screen with each box labeled with a participant's name. Invite everyone to use the annotation tool to add a reflection to their box.

Reflection questions could include:
- What will you do differently because of this training course?
- What system or product will you change when you return to work?
- What is your key takeaway from this activity?
- What is one thing you found valuable today?

When every box is filled, invite participants to use a stamp tool to highlight ideas they appreciated or found insightful.

If your learning platform doesn't offer annotation, you could ask participants to share one-word responses using a digital engagement platform such as Slido or Mentimeter.

Step-by-Step Instructions

1. Share a PowerPoint slide with a box for each participant.
2. Ask them to use the annotation tool to add their comment—a phrase or a single word—to their box.
3. If annotation is unavailable to anyone, suggest that participants add their comments to chat and the facilitator or producer will add them to the appropriate box.
4. When boxes are filled, invite everyone to use a stamp tool to mark the ideas that resonate with them.
5. Save a screenshot to provide to everyone after the activity.
6. Ask a few quick debriefing questions if time allows.

Facilitator's Guide

What to Say	What to Do
We are going to do a quick reflection about your learning experience.	
On the screen, you'll find your name. In your box, please use the annotation tool to write one sentence to answer the question.	Select your reflection question. Display it on the screen at the top of your name grid slide.
If annotation isn't available to you, please leave your response in the chat.	
Once you've written down your thought, please read the others. Use the stamp tool to acknowledge the thoughts that resonate with you.	Monitor the time.
Wrap up the thought you are on.	
Look at what resonates with you.	
What stands out for you?	Consider a longer debrief if responses and time merit it.

How to Increase the Value

- Use Google Docs or share a document in Teams or a similar social channel to reflect in a shared digital space.
- Save the Fill In Your Box activity as a PDF to make it accessible to everyone after class.

Why I Like This Activity

Fill In Your Box has worked well for me with quiet groups because they are more likely to respond when given dedicated time and space. The activity also provides me with a clearer perspective on what ideas stand out for everyone.

I always like to take a screenshot of the group's work and share it with them after class.

Give It a Try

Add your name to the box provided. Write one sentence to describe a takeaway from what you've read in this book so far.

Fill In Your Box

> **NOW ASK YOURSELF**
>
> - When could you use Fill In Your Box?
> - Which participants would this reflection work well for?
> - What challenges could this activity present?
> - How could you modify Fill In Your Box to fit your typical training course?

Draw Your Thought

Does drawing make you nervous? Don't turn the page just yet! Give this drawing activity a chance. We usually spend hours each day writing about, reading about, and discussing ideas, but most of us rarely consider drawing pictures of our thoughts. Drawing our thoughts can benefit anyone, not just artists.

Although drawing isn't typical in most work environments, I've found that doodling and sketching can be valuable reflection tools. People tend to remember images better than words, a phenomenon known as the "picture-superiority effect." Drawing can also help clarify complex topics that are difficult to express verbally.

Researchers have found that "drawing to-be-learned information significantly enhances memory performance, with greater gains than other mnemonic techniques" (Fernandes et al. 2018). This activity uses reflective drawing to help increase information retention.

AT A GLANCE

Reflection Type
- Individual response, private

Delivery Method
- Virtual instructor-led training
- Instructor-led training
- E-learning
- Self-directed learning

Number of Participants
- Any number

Time Needed
- 5–7 minutes

Reflection Timing
- During
- After

The Activity

Participants are invited to consider everything they've learned in their program and to draw pictures of their key learning points.

No one passes judgment on anyone else's drawing skills. Suggest participants describe their drawings with descriptive labels if they can't recognize what they've drawn (my drawings of the brain often look like cauliflower). Provide an example to help get everyone started. When everyone is finished drawing, you can invite participants to share what they've drawn.

Step-by-Step Instructions

1. At the midway point or conclusion of your program, ask everyone to find a space where they can draw easily and provide a blank sheet of paper. If meeting virtually, consider using a shared whiteboard.
2. Ask participants to think about key points they want to remember and implement when they return to work.
3. After two minutes, ask them to draw out one or more of their points.
4. Encourage them to continue to refine and add visual information to t heir drawings.

Facilitator's Guide

What to Say	What to Do
We are going to do a little reflection through drawing.	
Yes, even you can do a little drawing. No artistry is required, and I won't ask you to share if you don't want to.	
Take a moment and think about the key points or actions from our time together.	Set a 2-minute timer.
Now that you've thought about them, please draw images for those key points.	Clarify any questions. Consider providing an example.
Thanks for taking time to reflect.	
I challenge you to keep adding to your drawing as you learn more.	

How to Increase the Value

- Provide pictures of key points during the training session. Ask everyone to consider how the visual images help clarify the points. Later in the session, invite everyone to draw the original images from memory.
- Encourage doodling and sketching from the beginning of your program. Provide markers, crayons, or colored pencils. Leave doodling space in workbooks. Encourage a sense of play so participants can have fun with the assignment.
- Consider using the Piccles app, which uses three steps to lead simple reflection:
  - Ask a prompt question.
  - Draw the answer.
  - Analyze group responses.

> **PROVIDE OPTIONS**
>
> To make this activity accessible for everyone, provide clear, step-by-step instructions and offer drawing alternatives. Options might include writing descriptive words, verbally describing an image, or even molding clay. Before beginning, discuss preferences and creative approaches with participants.

Why I Like This Activity

I first asked participants to draw to fill an unexpected gap while we waited for everyone to arrive for a class. I was surprised how willing people were to draw using virtual annotation and how much lightness and laughter it brought to class.

I now ask people to draw in response to questions when they return from breaks, when we review previous content, and when we reflect at the conclusion of class. Figure 5-3 is an example of a drawing from a virtual class. Participants were first asked to recall the best practices, then I revealed the images and words we'd used during class for comparison.

Figure 5-3. Drawings of Best Practices for a Virtual Classroom

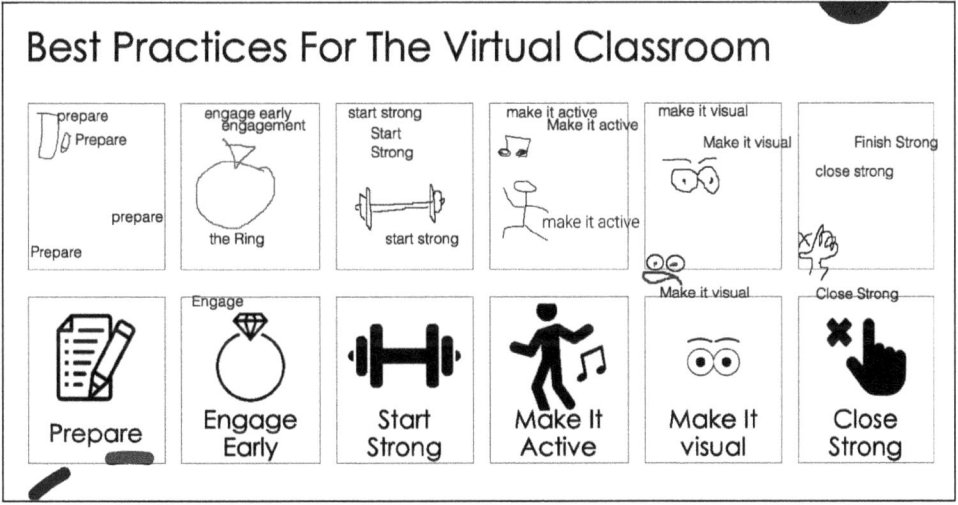

Give It a Try

Think of something you want to recall from the reading so far or from a recent conversation. Draw an image of it. Make sure to set any self-criticism aside!

Draw Your Thought Here!

NOW ASK YOURSELF

- When could you use Draw Your Thought?
- Which participants would this work well for?
- What concepts or ideas could you illustrate in simple line drawings?

What's It Like?

What is reading this book like? Is the experience enjoyable, like a walk in the park? Or is it as unpleasant as a trip to the dentist for a root canal?

Think about those three questions. Did each one create a different mental image? Each question used a *simile*, a figure of speech that compares two things, usually using the word *like* or *as*. Similes provide a way for us to compare what we are learning to something we already know. Similes also provide context we can relate to, making information more memorable. They can be a lighthearted approach to reflection that works especially well in groups.

Here are a few examples I've shared in classes:

- De-escalating anger is like watching a wind-up toy lose energy. We just need to wait it out.
- Needs assessment is like preparing to go to the grocery store; we take stock of what we have, consider the meals needed for the people in our home, and make a list of what we will need.

AT A GLANCE

Reflection Type
- Individual response, private
- Individual response, publicly shared
- Paired response, publicly shared
- Small group response, publicly shared

Delivery Method
- Virtual instructor-led training
- Instructor-led training

Number of Participants
- Any number
- The more people involved, the more time will be required

Time Needed
- 3–5 minutes for simile writing
- 5 additional minutes for discussing similes

Reflection Timing
- During
- After

The Activity

Ask everyone to create a simile (*x* is like *y*) to describe their training experience or an activity they've experienced. Make sure to provide a few examples. Consider asking people to work together in small groups.

When everyone is ready, post the similes in a shared space. Ask everyone to indicate which ones stand out and why.

Step-by-Step Instructions

1. Share a few examples of similes. Here are two that may inspire you:
   - Completing compliance training is like flossing your teeth—not much fun, but it helps you avoid problems in the future.
   - Managing people is like tending a garden—it requires nourishment, patience, and the right climate.
2. Ask everyone to write a simile describing their learning experience.
3. Give everyone a few minutes to write their similes.
4. Invite them to share what they've written with a small group or display them in a shared space.

Facilitator's Guide

What to Say	What to Do
You are all probably familiar with similes. These are phrases that compare something to something else using the word like or as. For example, you might say, "Compliance training is like flossing your teeth—not much fun, but it helps you avoid problems in the future."	
Creating similes can help you remember key concepts from class. They create a mental image you can recall after our time together.	
Here are a few more examples to help inspire you.	Provide a few examples.
Take a few minutes to write your similes. I'll ask a few of you to share yours with the room.	Clarify any questions and monitor time.
Who would like to share their similes?	Invite several responses as time allows.
Thanks for taking the time to reflect on today's class with your similes.	

How to Increase the Value

- Ask everyone to create a statement at the beginning of training and at the end. Compare the two.
- Debrief the activity with reflection questions.
- Share similes in a shared location, such as on Padlet, FigJam, or Miro.

Why I Like This Activity

The power of this activity lies in each individual's thought process and creativity.

When responses are funny or unusual, I often ask, "What prompted your simile?" This is one reflection activity that almost always gets a chuckle or two. Some of my favorites from recent training programs include:

- This training course was like going to a museum with a really great map.
- Retrieval practice is like Mary Poppins pulling things out of her bag.
- This class was like a breath of fresh air, helping me realize I'm not alone.

Give It a Try

Think of your experience reading this book. Use the space provided to describe what it is like in just a sentence or two.

Reading This Book Is Like. . . .

NOW ASK YOURSELF

- When could you use What's It Like?
- What groups would this reflection work well for?
- Which participants would it not work well for?
- How could you alter What's It Like? to fit programs you design or deliver?

Conclusion

Learning is difficult. This is a statement that won't surprise anyone reading this book. Learning always takes effort and time, but retrieval and reflection can help make learning happen more easily.

Using reflection and retrieval, we can help people remember important concepts during and after training. Just a few minutes of reflection at spaced intervals throughout a learning experience create long-lasting effects on memory. We are much more likely to remember details, processes, and procedures after we've put some effort into thinking about what we've experienced, tied our experiences to our existing knowledge, used a different skill set to create a drawing, or considered what actions we can take when we return to the workplace.

Reflection provides the time people need to create stronger neural pathways so they can retrieve information when they need it back on the job. The more effortful we make reflection, the more people will be able to retrieve over time.

In this chapter, you learned six ways to strengthen memory.

- **Five Bullets:** A quick activity that asks participants to identify five key takeaways or actions from the learning experience
- **One Question:** An exercise that has people write and reflect on their own questions about the content, encouraging deeper engagement and revealing areas of uncertainty
- **The Spinning Wheel of Wonder:** A novel approach using a digital spinning wheel to randomly select reflection questions for group discussion
- **Fill In Your Box:** An activity that has participants add brief reflections to a personalized box on a shared screen
- **Draw Your Thought:** Enhances memory retention through the creation of simple drawings that represent key concepts
- **What's It Like?:** Fosters creative reflection and memorable connections through similes that compare participants' learning experiences or concepts to familiar ideas

FINAL QUESTIONS FOR REFLECTION

- What do you want to recall from this chapter?
- Which activities will be most useful in your own design and delivery?

Chapter 6
Outcome 4: Create Deeper Insight

> The reason people get good ideas in the shower is because it's the only time during the day when most people are away from screens long enough to think clearly. The lesson is not to take more showers, but rather to make more time to think.
>
> —James Clear, author, *Atomic Habits*

How often do you jump to the easy answer? Have you ever found yourself quickly answering a question only to realize later that you were wrong and should have taken more time before responding?

In his popular 2011 book, *Thinking, Fast and Slow*, Daniel Kahneman runs an experiment asking people to solve what appears to be a simple math equation. A baseball bat and a ball cost $1.10 together. The bat costs $1 more than the ball. How much does the ball cost? The first time I read this, like many people, I quickly answered in my head: *Of course, the ball costs 10 cents*. I didn't realize my mistake until I read further and then stopped to consider the question more intentionally. In fact, the bat cost $1.05 and the ball cost five cents. Once you pause to think about it, the answer becomes obvious.

Deeper insight into any question or concept always requires time and effort. When we highlight people's existing knowledge, we help build confidence, and that confidence can help foster deeper understanding and more meaning. That's the type of reflection we'll encourage with the activities in this chapter.

Make New Connections

I like to imagine that when I pause to think about a new concept, I'm gathering my existing knowledge from various parts of my memory. Connecting new ideas to our existing knowledge is an essential step for deeper learning. Many people do this naturally, but some don't. Giving participants a little nudge through intentional reflection can help them connect their new experiences to their older experiences. When they make that connection, their learning becomes more durable.

A nudge doesn't have to be difficult; sometimes it's as simple as suggesting that everyone stop to think for a moment. We can ask questions like "How is this like something else you've experienced?" "What does this mean?" or "What is the value of this?" To create even deeper insight, we can guide participants with more difficult questions that engage their natural curiosity.

As Stefaan van Hooydonk (2022) explains in *The Workplace Curiosity Manifesto*, "Curiosity needs knowledge to build on, and the more knowledge we have, the more questions we can ask and inferences we can make."

QUICK QUESTIONS: REFLECTION IN ACTION

Use these questions when you want to deepen understanding of a concept but haven't planned a reflection activity. Use one or two, depending on how much time you have. Replace the word "this" with a specific activity or topic you've covered.

- What is the value of this?
- What are the benefits of this?
- What does this mean for you? For your work?
- What questions could you ask about this?
- How would you explain this to a five-year-old?

Activities

We unlock deeper insights through deliberate, effortful reflection. This chapter provides activities that connect participants' existing knowledge to new ideas, challenging them to create connections through both analogies and comparisons. Through these activities, participants will develop thoughtful questions and explore their curiosity.

Take Two Minutes

Do you have two minutes to spare in your next training program? I bet you can find it. Reflection takes time, but it doesn't have to take an extended period. With a well-chosen question or prompt, participants can deepen their insight and create more durable learning. A quick two-minute reflection activity is accessible for novice reflectors and also benefits seasoned reflectors.

Begin with one specific question that everyone can think about for two minutes. They can talk, write, or just think. Consider your participants' needs and preferences when you choose the method, providing them with options when possible. Knowing how long they will be asked to reflect helps people focus and write with intention. Two minutes is enough time for most people to pause, think, and document actions they want to remember when they return to work. It's a quick cognitive shift and can provide a transition to other activities or content.

Take Two Minutes works well during training and as a final reflection. I like to use it multiple times throughout a program.

AT A GLANCE

Reflection Type
- Individual response, private
- Individual response, shared anonymously
- Individual response, publicly shared

Instructional Format
- Virtual instructor-led training
- Instructor-led training
- E-learning
- Self-directed learning

Number of Participants
- Any number

Time
- 2 minutes
- (Optional) 3–5 minutes for discussion

Reflection Timing
- During
- After

The Activity

First, alert everyone that you are going to take two minutes for a quick reflection activity. Provide a question or prompt for them to consider. Encourage everyone to write down their responses. Let everyone know they are not required to share their responses.

Try one of these questions:
- What is the value of what we've covered today?
- How do these ideas relate to what you already know?
- What's an example of this concept in your own experience?

- What was this activity like?
- How can you use this information in your work?

Step-by-Step Instructions
1. Explain that everyone will take two minutes to respond to a reflection question.
2. Suggest that they write their reflection down somewhere they can reference it later, either on paper or digitally.
3. Set a two-minute timer.
4. Ask them to begin writing.
5. At the end of two minutes, ask everyone to finish the thought they are on.
6. Thank them for taking time to reflect.

Facilitator's Guide

What to Say	What to Do
Reflection is a powerful tool. It helps us solidify what we've learned by transferring it to our long-term memory.	
To help with this process, take two minutes to answer the question, "What is the value of what we've covered so far?" *[Or any other reflection question.]* This is a private reflection, and you don't have to share it with anyone.	Show the question slide.
I'll set a two-minute timer and give you a warning when we have 30 seconds remaining.	Set a two-minute timer.
You have 30 seconds remaining.	
Go ahead and wrap up the idea you are on.	
Thanks for taking time to reflect on your experience.	

How to Increase the Value
- Ask each person to keep their two-minute reflections in a document or notebook that they can return to throughout class.
- Take time at the end of your session to ask everyone to review their own reflections.
- If your group is reluctant to reflect, consider including a step that invites them to share reflections in small groups. Let them know from the start that they will have the option of sharing, which could be the nudge they need to reflect. However, don't *require* sharing.

- Avoid using words like *most, best, least,* or *favorite* in your question. These words require people to judge their experience more critically, which can take longer than two minutes.
- Build in two minutes of reflection after critical points in e-learning modules. Consider incorporating a two-minute timer with quiet music that participants can choose to mute.
- If you are working with a group of people who enjoy reflection, consider increasing the two minutes to three.

Why I Like This Activity

This activity fits almost any schedule or type of content! It's enough time to do a little thinking without creating a long, awkward space for those reluctant to reflect. I see the greatest benefit when I include two-minute reflections multiple times throughout training. Participants can look back at their reflections, build on them, and see the depth of their understanding increase over time.

I've never had anyone complain about pausing to stop and process what they are thinking. It provides a strategic pause that benefits everyone.

Give It a Try

Take two minutes to respond to the question in the space provided.

> What do you now know about reflection that you didn't know before starting this book?

NOW ASK YOURSELF

- When could you use Take Two Minutes?
- Which participants would this activity work well for?
- How could you alter Take Two Minutes to fit your training programs?

R&R

This activity is about *retrieval* and *reflection* (not rest and relaxation!). You've probably noticed by this point that retrieval and reflection often go hand in hand. We look back on what we've experienced and then determine our actions moving forward. This activity asks participants to retrieve a list of ideas or concepts they've covered. After they've retrieved those ideas, the reflection begins. By the end, they will be better prepared to transfer their learning to the workplace because they've developed and documented a deeper understanding of the material.

The following example shows how I used R&R after attending a conference session with Sarah Mercier, editor of *Design for All Learners* (2025). This short, personal activity helped me move Sarah's ideas to action.

Example R&R: Creating Accessible Documents

List three things you can recall from class:
- Use alt text.
- Describe the link instead of "click here."
- Don't use color to convey meaning.

Identify three actions you can take to implement what you've recalled:
- Edit PowerPoint slides to include alt text.
- Use the accessibility checker in PowerPoint and Word to identify changes I need to make.
- Going forward, check the color usage and contrast in my PowerPoint decks.

AT A GLANCE

Reflection Type
- Individual response, private
- Individual response, publicly shared
- Paired response, private
- Paired response, publicly shared
- Small group response, private
- Small group response, publicly shared

Instructional Format
- Virtual instructor-led training
- Instructor-led training
- E-learning
- Self-directed learning

Number of Participants
- Any number

Time
- 6–8 minutes

Reflection Timing
- During
- After

The Activity

Ask everyone to list, on paper or in a digital document, three things they can remember from training. They can choose any level of detail that works for them.

After they've finished the retrieval process, ask them to reflect on specific actions they could take using the information they've recalled. Optionally, participants can share their R&R results in small groups or with the entire group.

Step-by-Step Instructions

1. Let everyone know you are going to conduct a two-part activity. First they will *retrieve*, and then they will *reflect*.
2. Ask participants to consider everything covered in class up to this point.
3. Give them three minutes to write down three things they can remember from class.
4. After three minutes, ask them to reflect on their list and identify three specific actions they can take at work.
5. Ask for a few volunteers to share their lists.

Facilitator's Guide

What to Say	What to Do
I'm going to lead you through a two-part activity to retrieve information you've experienced and to reflect on how you can use the information.	
Take the next three minutes to write down three things you can recall from class. They can be very specific or general.	Provide paper if needed. Monitor the group to determine when everyone has finished.
Now, review your list. Consider what actions you can take at work, based on that list. Let's now take another three minutes to write down three actions you can take.	Monitor the time.
It's now been three minutes. Let's take a moment to hear a few of your ideas.	Hear perspectives from several people. Discuss as much as time permits.
Thank you!	

How to Increase the Value
- Repeat the reflection throughout your training, asking everyone to collect their information in one location so they can easily find it.
- Instead of asking for volunteers to share their lists at the end of the activity, put participants in pairs or small groups to discuss their responses.
- Invite everyone to share their reflection with their manager when they return to work.

Why I Like This Activity
I like tying the retrieval of information to reflection to help people see the relevance of the time and effort they've invested in learning. Breaking the activity into two parts helps people distinguish between what they *know* and what they *are going to do*. When participants share their R&R lists with me, I can see what resonates with them and where I might need to provide more support both during and after training.

I was inspired by what José Bueno, a California Conservation Corps member, shared about this activity: "The more we reach back into our minds and remember, the more we put it to use, and the more efficient we become."

Give It a Try
Consider this book or an article you've read related to learning. In the space provided, identify three things you can recall and three actions you can take based on what you learned.

Three things I can recall:

1. _____

2. _____

3. _____

Three actions I can take to implement what I've recalled:

1. _____

2. _____

3. _____

NOW ASK YOURSELF

- When could you use R&R?
- Which participants would benefit most from this activity?
- How could you alter this activity to fit your training programs?

Instructional Origami

Want to engage participants in a unique way while they reflect? Instructional Origami is a fun answer. In our digitally driven world, a simple piece of paper can become a novel reflection method. We're all creatures of the keyboard these days, so using a "vintage" method tends to grab people's attention. I must admit that I didn't create the name of this activity. The credit belongs to Britt Keahey, a participant in one of my workshops for trainers. She jokingly called it "instructional origami"—and the name stuck!

There are smiles every time I ask people to fold a piece of paper. In one training, someone shared with me that she loved having a dedicated spot to take notes throughout training. Her paper was filled at the end of our five-week training program.

Like all the activities, there's science behind this one. Writing with a pen and paper has a strong, positive effect on memory (Roberts and Wammes 2021). A physical piece of paper can be easily referenced during a learning experience and becomes a powerful reminder in each person's work area. I share a threefold version in Figure 6-1, but you can get creative by using a variety of different folds and prompts.

Figure 6-1. Instructional Origami

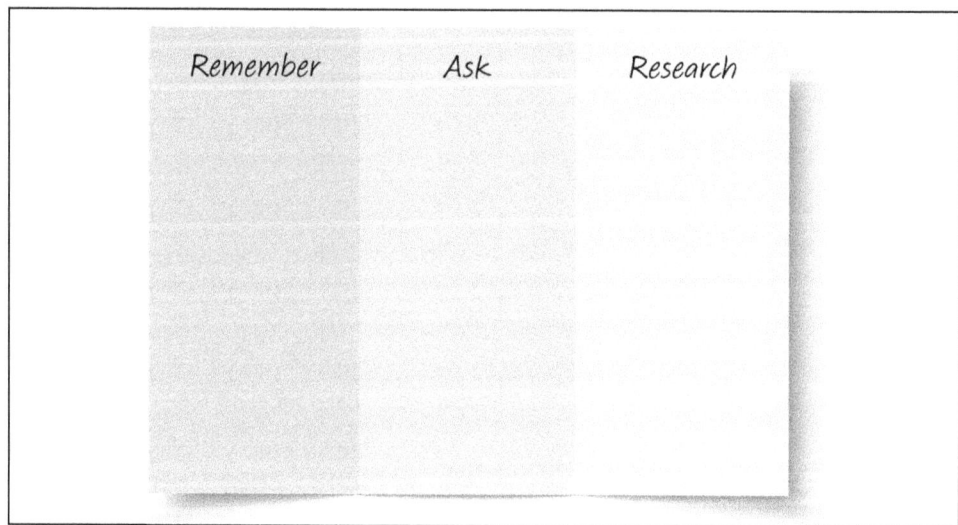

AT A GLANCE

Reflection Type
- Individual response, private

Instructional Format
- Virtual instructor-led training
- Instructor-led training
- E-learning
- Self-directed learning

Number of Participants
- Any number

Time
- 15–21 minutes, dispersed in 3-minute sections throughout an experience

Reflection Timing
- Before
- During
- After

The Activity

You'll distribute a sheet of paper (colorful or plain) to each participant or ask them to grab one from their recycle pile. They will need only one blank side.

Ask each participant to fold their sheet into three columns and label each column *Remember, Ask,* and *Research*. They'll then write down their thoughts in each column throughout the program.

Step-by-Step Instructions

1. Announce a reflection activity at the beginning of training.
2. Distribute a sheet of 8.5x11 paper to everyone or ask them to get their own. It can be recycled because they will use only one side.
3. Demonstrate folding the paper in thirds, like mailing a letter in an envelope.
4. Ask participants to label each column with the words *Remember, Ask,* and *Research*.
5. Invite them to use the paper throughout training to write down what they want to remember, ask, or research outside class.
6. Take a few minutes, at spaced intervals throughout training, for reflection.
7. At the end of training, ask everyone to review their reflections.

Facilitator's Guide

What to Say	What to Do
Grab a piece of printer paper. Recycled paper is OK. We are going to use only one side of it.	Hold up a sheet of paper as an example.
We are going to fold the paper into thirds, like you are mailing a letter.	Demonstrate folding the paper into thirds.
Unfold your paper and you will have three columns.	Hold up the paper showing three columns.
Label the first column *Remember*. Here you'll write anything you want to remember as we move through class.	
Label the second column *Ask*. Write anything you want to talk to me, your manager, or a peer about, either in person or via email.	
Label the third column *Research*. Here you'll jot down ideas you would like to do more research on later.	
Throughout our time together I'll stop and ask you to reflect on the thoughts recorded on your paper. Keep it close to capture your ideas anytime you'd like.	
Let's take three minutes now to reflect on your experiences so far.	Set a 3-minute timer.
We'll come back to this activity throughout our time together.	Return to the paper at regular intervals during class, asking people to continue adding to it.

How to Increase the Value

- Debrief the experience. At the end of the class, say, "I'd love to hear three things that you've reflected on. Who would like to share the first one?"
- Try the same activity with slightly different approaches to the origami or columns:
    - *Eight or 16 squares:* Fold the paper into eight or 16 squares and ask participants to fill the boxes with ideas they can recall from class and actions they will take after class.
    - *Four Corners:* Use the paper-folding method described in the Four Corners activity.

Why I Like This Activity

I love the novelty and hands-on nature of folding paper. It's reminiscent of when we made "cootie catchers" in junior high—the multi-folded papers that could be manipulated to reveal our future.

I often see a lot of satisfaction on people's faces when they hold a single sheet of paper filled with their own thoughts at the end of class.

Give It a Try

Grab a piece of paper and fold it into thirds, which will become three columns. Write Remember, Ask, and Research at the top of each column. Take a moment to record what you want to remember, ask (via email or in person), and research about this book.

Come back to this page while you finish the book. You may use the space provided to record your thoughts, but it won't be as fun as folding a separate sheet of paper!

Remember	Ask	Research

NOW ASK YOURSELF

- When could you use Instructional Origami?
- What programs would this work well for?
- What other labels could you give each column?

Four Corners

Have you noticed that gaining deeper insight through reflection often includes thinking from multiple perspectives? Considering an experience from multiple perspectives helps reveal what we might otherwise miss if we asked only a single question.

Four Corners asks everyone to reflect on their learning experience from four different perspectives. This method works well individually, but its value increases when conducted in groups. Start individually and end with group reflection whenever possible.

AT A GLANCE

Reflection Type
- Individual response, private
- Individual response, publicly shared
- Small group response, publicly shared
- Large group response

Instructional Format
- Virtual instructor-led training
- Instructor-led training
- E-learning
- Self-directed learning

Number of Participants
- Any number

Time Needed
- 5–10 minutes

Reflection Timing
- After

The Activity

In this activity, participants reflect on training content based on four themes or perspectives: *I liked, I learned, I want,* and *I will*. They first reflect individually on the themes. After their initial reflection, they can identify one item from each area to share in a small group or with the whole group.

Consider using Four Corners throughout training, inviting everyone to add their thoughts as training progresses.

Step-by-Step Instructions

1. Provide everyone with a blank piece of paper to be folded into four quadrants. If you are in a virtual training, consider using a shared Whiteboard or Google Doc.
2. Explain that everyone will have 10 minutes to reflect on each area. Encourage them to write as much as they want for each of the four topics.
3. Provide a quick example of what you might write in each area.

4. Set a 10-minute timer.
5. At the 10-minute mark, or when everyone appears to be done, invite them to finish the item they are on.
6. If time allows, ask people to share examples from each of the quadrants.

Facilitator's Guide

What to Say	What to Do
Let's do a quick reflection activity.	Give everyone an 8.5x11 piece of paper.
Fold your paper in half and then in half again.	Demonstrate folding the paper.
Open your paper. You'll notice four quadrants. We are now going to name each quadrant: • The upper left quadrant is labeled "I Liked." • The upper right is labeled "I Learned." • The bottom left is "I Want." • The bottom right is "I Will."	Provide a visual example, with one answer in each quadrant.
Now that you've got everything labeled, let's take the next few minutes to consider each quadrant. Write down anything that comes to mind for you.	Monitor time and clarify any questions.
Thanks for taking time to reflect. I'd encourage you to return to your paper and add anything you'd like as we move through class together.	

How to Increase the Value
- Lead a large group discussion asking for highlights from each quadrant.
- For in-person programs, post four charts in the four corners of your space. Write one statement on each sheet. Split your group into four, sending each group to one of the four corners or rotating to each corner, adding to the reflection as they rotate.
- Form small groups to discuss and add their insights to each quadrant.

Why I Like This Activity

I love seeing how the four statements appeal to different people. Some people enjoy looking back, others benefit from looking forward, and still others prefer asking deeper questions about the meaning of the experience. None are wrong.

This is also a very flexible activity. The four statements can be renamed to better fit a specific group or program. I love to watch what happens in a physical space where people can move around and see what others have written. It also works well virtually.

Give It a Try

In the space provided, consider your experience reading this book. Take a few minutes to reflect and add your thoughts to each quadrant.

I Liked	I Learned
I Want	I Will

> **NOW ASK YOURSELF**
> - When could you use Four Corners?
> - Whom would this reflection work well for?
> - How could you adapt this activity to fit your training program?

Before and After

We all arrive to training with a set of expectations about what we will learn. Those expectations often change by the end of training because our perspective shifts as we gain new information. This activity asks people to identify what they know about a topic before a learning experience and then compare it with what they have learned by the end. This reflection on reflection can reveal the degree of learning someone has experienced as well as opportunities for further learning.

AT A GLANCE

Reflection Type
- Individual response, private
- Individual response, publicly shared

Instructional Format
- Virtual instructor-led training
- Instructor-led training

Number of Participants
- Any number

Time
- 7–10 minutes

Reflection Timing
- Before
- During
- After

The Activity

As you begin, everyone writes a list of the things they know about the topic you are going to cover. They then set the paper or digital document aside until the end of the program. At the end, you'll invite everyone to return to their Before and After document to write everything they now know. Ask participants to compare what they've written.

Step-by-Step Instructions

1. At the beginning of a program, ask everyone to find a place to write down their reflections for this activity (on paper or digitally).
2. Invite them to reflect on what they know about the topic before you dive into the content.
3. Provide a list of learning objectives to spark ideas and set a timer for five minutes.
4. At the conclusion of the program, ask everyone to return to their Before and After paper or digital document.
5. Ask participants to review the Before list.
6. Invite them to write down everything they have learned in the After space.

Facilitator's Guide

What to Say	What to Do
Please write on a piece of paper or a digital document that you can easily return to throughout our program.	
Review the objectives and content we are exploring together.	Provide participants with learning objectives or a course outline.
Take the next five minutes to write down everything you know about each of the topics listed. It's OK to take guesses or pull from related ideas. You can't be wrong with this.	Set a 5-minute timer.
Finish the thought you are on.	Pause while everyone finishes.
Would a few people like to share some things they wrote down?	Hear from 3 or 4 participants.
(At the conclusion of the program): Let's look back at what you wrote down at the beginning of class.	Pause to let people find their digital or paper documents.
In the After column, now write what you know, what has changed, or what you've added to your knowledge about this topic.	
Would a few people like to share some things they wrote down?	Hear responses from 3 or 4 participants.

How to Increase the Value

- Provide a piece of paper to fold, as in Instructional Origami. Label one half *Before* and one half *After*.
- Consider providing an explicit Before and After template, with each learning objective or outcome listed.
- Add small group discussions at the beginning and end of the activity.

Why I Like This Activity

Taking an inventory of what we know is often highly motivating. Adding to that inventory in a meaningful way builds confidence.

I love when people can check things off their list that they knew, and when people have that light-bulb moment when they see things differently from before.

I also love the joy I heard from one participant, who said, "I know so much more than when I started!"

Give It a Try

Review the reflection learning outcomes listed in the introduction of this book. In the space provided, write down what you believed before starting. Return after you've finished to record your "after."

Learning Outcomes	Before	After
		What I Knew What Changed What I Learned

NOW ASK YOURSELF

- When could you use Before and After?
- What types of training programs would this work well for?
- How could you alter this activity to fit your training programs?

What? Gut? So What? Now What?

Debriefing is my favorite form of reflection. I learned this debriefing method from Sivasailam "Thiagi" Thiagarajan, an L&D game guru and author. Thiagi emphasizes that "the learning is in the debrief." I'd add that debriefing itself is a form of reflection. His method purposefully walks people through their experience, from what they initially notice to actionable insights in the workplace.

Debriefing has a variety of formats and names. The Institute of Cultural Affairs calls it "focused conversation," while John Driscoll (a renowned healthcare educator and reflective practice theorist) developed what he called the "What?" method. In addition, the 3D model of Debriefing follows a similar structure as Thiagi's to defuse, discover, and deepen reflection on an experience.

Some approaches skip the "Gut?" question, but I believe exploring our emotional responses to an experience is important. Understanding how people feel helps determine preferences and usually leads to richer, deeper discussions.

AT A GLANCE

Reflection Type
- Individual response, publicly shared
- Large group response

Instructional Format
- Virtual instructor-led training
- Instructor-led training
- E-learning
- Self-directed learning

Number of Participants
- Any number

Time
- 5–10 minutes

Reflection Timing
- During
- After

The Activity

Through a series of questions, people reflect on an activity, an objective, or their overall training experience. Each initial question leads to another deeper question. While this activity typically takes place as a group discussion, you can also use it as a written reflection.

Begin by determining your focus. You might focus on an activity after it's completed. You might focus on a portion of training during a multipart training course. Keep the same focus as you ask each of the questions.

As you ask the questions, avoid adding your own thoughts or critique. Let this reflection be the participants' unique experience. Sitting with silence is important for debriefing so reflection can occur. The questions include:

- What stood out for you about [*the focus of your conversation*]?

- What was easy about [*the focus of your conversation*]?
- What was difficult about [*the focus of your conversation*]?
- What was the value of [*the focus of your conversation*]?
- What will you do differently going forward?

Step-by-Step Instructions
1. Let everyone know you are going to lead a debrief discussion.
2. Ask the first question.
3. Wait for responses.
4. Consider repeating your question as you originally asked it. Avoid rewording it unless there is obvious confusion about the question.
5. Wait for more responses!
6. Repeat key points from each response. Don't add you own thoughts.
7. Ask the subsequent questions one at a time, pausing and repeating key points from each response. Avoid adding your own stories, opinions, or critique.
8. At the end, thank everyone for their contributions to the discussion.

Facilitator's Guide

What to Say	What to Do
We are going to debrief the activity we've just completed.	
I'll ask a series of questions, give you time to think, and then request your response.	
What stood out for you about the activity?	Wait for responses. Repeat key points from responses. Don't add your own thoughts to the discussion. After 3 to 4 responses, move to the next question.
What was easy about this activity?	Wait, repeat key points, and move to the next question.
What was difficult about this activity?	Wait, repeat key points, and move to the next question.
What was the value of this activity?	Wait, repeat key points, and move to the next question.
What will you do differently going forward at work because of this activity?	Wait, repeat key points, and move to the next question.
Thank you for a great conversation.	Answer any questions that may have come up during the discussion that were not answered by peers.

How to Increase the Value
- Provide everyone with the questions *before* your discussion. Give them time to consider each question. Then lead the discussion.
- Give the questions to small groups in breakout rooms. Ask them to discuss.
- Consider some variations of each question that best fit your group:
  - What did you notice during this activity?
  - What did you like about the activity?
  - What did you dislike about the activity?
  - What did you learn from the activity?
  - What action will you take because of the activity?

Why I Like This Activity
If you are looking for my most field-tested reflection activity, you've found it. I use this reflection method, or a variation of it, in every training course I facilitate. The "What have you noticed?" question is a safe, easy one that most people are comfortable responding to. Their responses can't be wrong. It primes everyone for deeper reflection in subsequent questions.

This activity can be used as a discussion or as individual written reflection. It's versatile, thorough, and effective. Be warned: Some groups will dive into deep conversations with these questions. Those are my favorite groups.

Give It a Try
Answer each question in the space provided.

What? What can you recall about reflection based on your reading of this book so far?

Gut? What do you find easy about reflection?

Gut? What do you find difficult about reflection?

So What? So what has been the value of learning about reflection in this book?

Now What? Now what will you do differently when you return to work?

NOW ASK YOURSELF

- When could you use What? Gut? So What? Now What?
- What types of training or training topics would this work well for?
- How could you adapt this activity to fit your training programs?
- What focus will you use for your questions?

Wonder Wall

Have you ever asked a question and found yourself stuck in awkward silence? The Wonder Wall is my answer to that silence. This activity asks participants to reflect on what they are curious about related to your topic because, for many people, expressing curiosity is safer than asking a question or making a statement. I usually find that an invitation to be curious elicits more responses than asking, "What questions do you have?"

If you are looking for a quick reflection activity that prods people to think about a topic, the Wonder Wall is the one you want.

AT A GLANCE

Reflection Type
- Individual response, shared anonymously (for anonymity, turn off virtual annotation naming)
- Individual response, publicly shared

Instructional Format
- Virtual instructor-led training
- Instructor-led training

Number of Participants
- 1–20
- Note: More than 20 can lead to a messy, unreadable wall

Time
- 5–10 minutes

Reflection Timing
- Before
- During
- After

The Activity

Provide a blank space on a whiteboard or slide with "I'm wondering. . ." written at the top. Invite everyone to use a virtual annotation tool to write what they are wondering; if in person, you could use a flipchart or sticky notes on a wall. You could also use an engagement tool like Slido, Miro, or Mentimeter to collect responses.

Step-by-Step Instructions

1. Write "I'm wondering. . ." on a blank slide, wall, whiteboard, or digital space for sharing ideas.
2. Display the statement for participants.
3. Invite everyone to use an annotation tool, a pen and sticky notes, or another method to share their "wonders."
4. Consider sharing an example of your wonder to get people started.

5. As people begin to post items, more will usually follow.
6. Once everyone's wonders have been posted, you can:
   - Discuss as many as you have time for.
   - Place participants in breakout rooms and ask them to discuss two or three wonders that interest them. You might also consider creating breakout rooms based on the wonders and letting people choose their breakout rooms.
   - Follow up after class with answers and resources for each of the wonders.
7. Keep in mind that some wonders are just that: things people are wondering about. They don't all need elaborate responses.

Facilitator's Guide

What to Say	What to Do
We are going to take a moment to see what you are wondering about our topic.	
This is the Wonder Wall. (Optional: Make a comment about finally discovering what Oasis was referring to. Consider playing part of the song for those unfamiliar with it.)	Share a whiteboard, flipchart, or blank PowerPoint slide—whatever method you choose. (Turn off virtual annotation naming if responses are to be anonymous.)
Take a moment to think about anything you are wondering about our topic. Write your "wonder" on the board [*or screen or slide*].	Show an example to get everyone started.
	Rearrange any wonders that overlap and place similar wonders together.
Thanks for adding your wonders. Let's take a moment to review a few.	
[*If working digitally*] Using your annotation tool, stamp the wonders you are most interested in exploring. [*If working in person*] Grab a marker. Place a check next to the wonders you are most interested in exploring.	Watch as everyone indicates common wonders.
What do you notice about the wonders?	Discuss the common wonders as time and your knowledge allow.
We have more wonders than we have time for today. I'll follow up after class with more information for each of the items you've listed here.	Take a screenshot to save the wonders or convert to a PDF. Follow up with resources or answers for the wonders after class.

How to Increase the Value
- Form breakout groups by wonders. Send people into rooms to discuss and return with insights for their assigned wonder.
- Create a resource referencing all the wonders. Consider using it for future training or distributing it to those who would benefit from it.
- Use a tool like Mentimeter or Slido to collect wonders. This will not have the visual punch or graffiti-like impact of the Wonder Wall but will offer people the opportunity to reflect.

Why I Like This Activity

If you ask a group of people, "What are your questions?" you might receive one or two responses. But if you say, "What are you wondering?" you'll open up the floodgates.

The first time I tried this activity, I held my breath and was amazed at the responses. It's now become a staple in my toolkit. I love when people share wonders I've never considered, and I use the wonders from one class to help improve later classes. They make me a better facilitator.

Inviting everyone to annotate their "wonders" to the wall proved to be safer, easier, and more fun for participants than many other approaches. The Wonder Wall also provides opportunities for humor or serious contemplation, depending on the participants' personalities. In any case, the reflections on the Wonder Wall can be a source of lively conversation, breakout group discussions, or helpful follow-up after class.

As a final note, my husband advised me not to share my opinion of the Oasis song in any way. So I'm taking his advice and just letting you know that we all now finally have an example of a Wonder Wall, something even the artists themselves claim to have no definition of! (Although I have it on good authority that it came from a George Harrison album, *Wonderwall Music*, which was the soundtrack for the movie *Wonderwall*.)

Give It a Try

In the space provided, take a few minutes to write everything you are wondering about reflection.

I'm wondering. . . .

NOW ASK YOURSELF

- When could you use the Wonder Wall?
- What types of training or training topics would this work well for?
- How could you alter the Wonder Wall to fit your training programs?

Tell Me a Story

We remember stories. We connect with one another through stories.

Stories matter.

Paul B. Armstrong (2020), who studies neuroscience and literature, writes that "stories help the brain negotiate the never-ending conflict between its need for pattern, synthesis, and constancy and its need for flexibility, adaptability, and openness to change."

This is why describing ideas to our peers in the form of stories is a powerful way to create clarity. We search for our words, pause to think, and formulate ideas. Hearing others go through the same process can reveal ideas we would not discover alone. Tell Me a Story invites small groups to tell a story about their understanding of a concept or learning experience. After sharing their stories, others respond with what they notice and value in the story before sharing their own.

AT A GLANCE

Reflection Type
- Paired response, private
- Paired response, publicly shared
- Small group response, private
- Small group response, publicly shared

Instructional Format
- Virtual instructor-led training
- Instructor-led training

Number of Participants
- 2 to many

Time
- 5–10 minutes

Reflection Timing
- During
- After

The Activity

Near the conclusion of training, ask everyone to take a moment to think about their experience. Form groups of three or four people and invite them to tell one another their stories about the experience. Reporting highlights back to the entire group is optional.

Step-by-Step Instructions

1. Ask everyone to think of a story they've heard, or a fairy tale, nursery rhyme, movie, or favorite book.
2. Point out how well stories stick with us, just like those they recalled.
3. Explain that you are going to use the power of stories to remember class content.
4. Invite everyone to think about their experience in class.

5. Ask them to imagine themselves a decade from now, reflecting on who they are today.
6. Ask them to think about what story they will tell the people around them.
7. Invite them to take a moment to write down what they think of. Make the exercise work for your participants. They can tell the entire story or just the key points, or even sketch it out as a storyboard.
8. Form small groups and ask everyone to share their stories.
9. If time allows, invite a few people to share stories with the entire group.

Facilitator's Guide

What to Say	What to Do
Do you have stories you can recall from your life? Maybe fairy tales or life moments? Favorite books?	Wait for and acknowledge a few answers.
Stories are memorable, so we're going to write stories of our experiences in this class. Remember that most stories have a moral or a call to action, so you may want to include something like that in your versions.	
Imagine it is 10 years from today and someone has asked you about your experience in this class.	
Take a few minutes to write your story. Use bullet points or complete paragraphs. You can also draw on a storyboard if that works for you.	Provide a storyboard template or a simple outline. Clarify questions or steps as needed.
We're now going to form small groups to share your stories. You'll have about 10 minutes.	Ensure that everyone is in a group and knows what to do.
Let's come back together. Thanks for sharing your stories.	Invite the groups back together after everyone has shared in their groups.

How to Increase the Value

- Debrief with the What? Gut? So What? Now What? activity.
- Record the stories on video or audio (with participants' permission) and send them to participants after class. Consider sharing stories (with permission) on Padlet or another app.
- If time permits, invite several people to volunteer to share stories with the entire group at the end of the activity.

Why I Like This Activity

Stories are personal, valuable, and memorable. I find that hearing stories shared by participants is always gratifying and often humorous. People share what works for them as well as where they struggle with implementing ideas.

Stories can help identify the support we can provide after a learning experience to ensure someone's success.

Give It a Try

Use the space provided to tell me a story about what you've read in this book or a conversation you've had about learning with a colleague.

My story is about. . . .

NOW ASK YOURSELF

- When could you use Tell Me a Story?
- What types of training or training topics would this work well for?
- How could you alter Tell Me a Story to fit your training programs?

Explain It to a Five-Year-Old

Have you ever tried to explain a difficult concept to a five-year-old? It's hard! They won't tolerate ambiguities or fluffy language. It's a struggle to find relatable words. It requires us to think about the world from a simpler point of view. It is reflection in action!

Reflection can provide clarity, but it can also be useful for consolidating and simplifying our ideas. Explain It to a Five-Year-Old provides an opportunity for simplification. The challenge of thinking about something from a different perspective, finding simple terms, and verbalizing our experience leads to deeper understanding.

AT A GLANCE

Reflection Type
- Paired response, private
- Paired response, publicly shared
- Small group response, private
- Small group response, publicly shared

Instructional Format
- Virtual instructor-led training
- Instructor-led training

Number of Participants
- 2 to many

Time
- 5–10 minutes

Reflection Timing
- During
- After

The Activity

At the conclusion of a learning event, ask everyone to think about their experience and imagine they need to explain to a five-year-old (or a room full of kindergartners!) what happened, what they learned, and what they will do differently on the job.

You may want to begin by asking everyone what qualities an explanation would need for a five-year-old to understand. Pair up participants after they've considered their responses and ask them to share with each other.

Step-by-Step Instructions

1. Ask everyone to imagine a five-year-old they know now or knew in the past.
2. Ask the group to suggest ways to communicate best with a five-year-old.
3. List the questions on a whiteboard, shared screen, or chart page.
4. Invite everyone to think about the learning objective or training content you've completed in terms a five-year-old would understand.

5. Ask participants to share their experience with a partner, as if they are explaining it to a five-year-old.
6. When everyone is done, invite members of the group to answer a few reflection questions:
    ◦ What stood out for you from the stories you shared?
    ◦ What was the value of explaining the experience to a five-year-old?

Facilitator's Guide

What to Say	What to Do
Can you imagine describing something to a five-year-old? That's exactly how we are going to reinforce your learning today.	
In a moment, I'll ask you to pair with someone. First, think of something you will do differently on the job, based on what we've learned in class. Explain that to each other as if you are speaking to a five-year-old. Be specific, descriptive, and ready for a five-year-old's questions.	
As examples, let's brainstorm some questions that five-year-olds might ask. Here are a few to get us started.	Display questions on a whiteboard or flipchart, or using another method. Ask for input from the participants in the class. A few initial questions would include: • Why? • How come? • Why do I have to? • What's that? • Can I do it?
Take a few minutes to think about what you might tell the five-year-old.	Provide any clarification needed.
Let's get in small groups so you can share your stories. You have 10 minutes.	Form groups of 2 or 3 people. Monitor time and give a time warning at the halfway point for groups to switch.
Thanks for sharing in your groups. I'd love to know what you noticed as you explained to each other.	

How to Increase the Value
- Ask everyone to record their explanations, adding them to a shared space such as Padlet or Flip.
- Record videos of the explanations. Send them to participants after class as an after-action reflection.
- Ask groups to ask questions in response to each story as if they are also five-year-olds.

Why I Like This Activity
We discover things about ourselves and what we are learning when we simplify things for other people, especially children. Explaining something to a five-year-old helps us reflect on our experience and glean the most important elements, removing the unnecessary.

I once watched someone struggle to find their five-year-old words. When they found the explanation that worked, they announced to everyone that they finally understood the concepts we had discussed.

Give It a Try
In the space provided, explain one thing you've learned about reflection as if you're speaking to a five-year-old.

I've learned. . . .

NOW ASK YOURSELF
- When could you use Explain It to a Five-Year-Old?
- What types of training or training topics would this work well for?
- How could you alter Explain It to a Five-Year-Old to fit your training programs?

Conclusion

Thinking more deeply is often about giving participants plenty of time to consider a few thoughtful questions that nudge their reflection forward. Which activities for thinking more deeply are you excited to use?

You have multiple methods to choose from to deepen participants' understanding, whether you want to connect their existing knowledge to new ideas or help them see applications for their experiences. Thinking more deeply about anything requires effort, but I find that the work always helps to create lasting learning.

In this chapter, you've explored activities for creating deeper understanding:

- **Take Two Minutes:** A quick two minutes of free-writing everything you can recall and its value
- **R&R:** Retrieving and reflecting work together; first, recall three things learned, and then reflect on what actions to take at work
- **Instructional Origami:** Paper-folding to identify three elements from a learning experience
- **Before and After:** An assessment of what you know about a topic, which you then compare with what you've learned by the program's conclusion
- **What? Gut? So What? Now What?** A four-part reflection framework used to dig deeper into any learning experience
- **Wonder Wall:** A blank wall that gets filled with everything participants are curious about as they explore a topic
- **Tell Me a Story:** Summing up a learning experience through shared stories for long-term retention
- **Explain It to a Five-Year-Old:** Distilling a learning experience to its essence by using simple language to help grasp the meaning

Consider ways to add reflection during training, but also create methods to prompt reflection after. Try sending a follow-up reflection question by email, or, if you have the technology available, use your learning management system or a text-based system. This drip-feeding after training can help deepen understanding and strengthen learning transfer to the workplace.

FINAL QUESTIONS FOR REFLECTION

Take a moment to reflect on what we've covered in this chapter. Here are some questions to help you reflect:

- What activities in this chapter best fit your participants, time, and desired outcome?
- How could you modify one of the activities to better meet your needs?
- What are you wondering about reflection?

Chapter 7
Outcome 5: Assess Progress

*Experiences have the most value
when you try to make sense of them.*
—Carole Robin, PhD, author, *Connect*

At any given moment, people have multiple distractions vying for their attention. How can you know when they understand a concept or when they've been pulled away by a work email or a Teams or Slack notification? Reflection can help you check in with participants and assess their progress, monitor their energy, and provide a mental break, reducing everyone's cognitive load.

Do a Pulse Check

I sometimes refer to assessing progress as taking a "pulse check." Pulse checks are quick moments of reflection interspersed throughout a learning experience (Figure 7-1). They can be used at the beginning of a program to gauge how people feel, or in the middle when it feels like energy and engagement might be waning. This gives you a sense of where people are and helps you modify your tone and direction. Participants also benefit when their feelings are acknowledged in the moment.

Figure 7-1. Assess Your Reading Energy

Are you still with me? How are you doing? Where would you put your reading energy on this scale?

Many participants in my training programs have shared their relief when I've followed difficult concepts with a moment of reflection. The pause gives them an opportunity to regroup and a much-needed break from additional information. Research suggests that we need space and time to process the information we encounter. In other words, short "brain breaks" are helpful for long-term retention (Lee et al. 2024).

By using the activities in this chapter at the beginning of a learning experience, you can assess readiness to learn with the bonus benefit of boosting participants' motivation.

By using the same activities in the middle of a learning experience, you can get a sense of how information is resonating with everyone and measure the group's engagement and energy levels. Plan to use pulse checks as opportunities for reflection in action (something we often skip) when you feel a group's energy dip.

Finally, you can return to the pulse check activities at the end of a learning experience to check progress one more time. Assessing progress from the beginning to the end of a training event can help identify when a program has gone well or when it's time for a redesign or more clarification.

> **QUICK QUESTIONS**
>
> Use these questions when you need something quick for everyone to reflect on. They'll help your group and give you a method to check everyone's pulse.
>
> - What can you do now that you couldn't do at the beginning of class?
> - What word describes your energy level?
> - What does this make you think of?
> - How are you feeling about this?
> - What are you frustrated with?

Activities

Most activities in this chapter are brief, taking two minutes or less. They are designed so the entire group can participate together. You can always expand any of the activities by adding discussion and additional reflection questions.

The Chat Cascade

Do you want to see a quick reflection response from everyone in your virtual program at once? The Chat Cascade is fast and produces a unique reflection from each participant. I use the word *cascade* because when you give the signal to press *enter*, everyone's words cascade onto the screen. This is great to use when time constraints make it difficult to include a longer reflection activity. Everyone shares their response at the same time, eliminating any copying of responses.

AT A GLANCE

Reflection Type
- Individual response, publicly shared

Delivery Method
- Virtual instructor-led training

Number of Participants
- 2 to many
- Consider using Slido, Mentimeter, or other digital presentation tools for more than 25 people

Time Needed
- 2–3 minutes

Reflection Timing
- During
- After

The Activity

Pose a reflection question related to your topic. Ask everyone to type their short answers into the chat but not to press *enter* until you give the go-ahead. After you've given everyone time to consider the question, do a NASA-style countdown and watch the chat explode with responses.

Ask everyone to read what has been shared. Highlight a few responses that stand out to you and ask which ones resonate most with the participants.

Here are a few reflective prompts you could consider using:
- How would you describe your experience in class?
- What stands out for you regarding this activity or objective?
- What is something you'll use from this class when you return to work?
- Write one word that describes how you are feeling now.
- Write two words to describe the most recent activity.
- Write a short phrase describing the value of what you've done today.
- Describe something from today's content that resonates with you.
- What is a phrase you've heard today that is sticking with you?

Step-by-Step Instructions

1. Explain that you would like everyone to reflect on their experience in class.
2. Share your reflection question.
3. Ask everyone to type their response in chat and then wait for your signal before they press enter.
4. Say something like, "There are 18 of you in class. I'd love to see 18 responses." I'm grateful to Cindy Huggett (2024) for this brilliant approach.
5. Give everyone time to write.
6. Count down 3-2-1 before saying, "Press enter!"
7. Watch a cascade of words fill the chat window.
8. Read a few of the responses or ask participants to share those that stand out most for them.

Facilitator's Guide

What to Say	What to Do
I want to take two minutes to check in with everyone.	
I'd like you to reflect on this statement.	Post your reflection statement onscreen or in chat.
Please type your response in the chat, but don't press enter until I say so.	
Type your response, and give me a nod when you're ready, but wait for my signal to hit enter.	
Wait . . .	Watch for signals that everyone is ready.
Three, two, one. . . . Press enter!	Read a few responses. Look for common threads or ideas to discuss.

How to Increase the Value

- Ask participants to point out the common themes they see in the responses. Ask, "What do you notice when you review all the words in the cascade?"
- Consider adding an improvised Chat Cascade to your programs as a pulse check when energy and engagement feel low.

Why I Like This Activity

I love the Chat Cascade! The speed of answers flying through the chat all at once makes everyone laugh and feel energized. Usually, responses will be just one or two words, and you will see responses from everyone.

I also love this activity because participants aren't prompted by what others have said. You'll get a few duplicates, but never the string of "dittos" or "what she saids" that you see in other activities. I've watched people light up when they discover shared responses.

Many people chime in with "I never thought of that!" after reading through their peers' responses.

What if someone presses enter too early? This happens, and all you need to do is remind them to wait, while acknowledging that hitting enter is an automatic, often unconscious response, and that it's OK.

Give It a Try

Doing this activity on your own won't have the cascade effect, but you'll still benefit from the reflection. Answer the questions in the space provided.

What three words would you use to describe your experience reading this book?
1. _____
2. _____
3. _____

NOW ASK YOURSELF

- When could you use the Chat Cascade?
- Whom would this reflection method work well for?
- How could you adapt this activity to fit your training program?

On a Scale of 1 to 5

If you've been to a public restroom in an airport or a restaurant chain, you might have taken part in a version of this reflection activity. Are you wondering what the heck I'm talking about?

Have you ever seen a strategically placed set of smiley faces—a smiley one, an indifferent one, and an angry one, strategically colored green, yellow, and red? For this activity, our reflection scale includes five points, not three, and you can use smiley and frowny faces or stars, or hold up one to five fingers—the options are endless. Use what will work best for your group. The point is to reflect quickly on what has been happening in class, with only a moment to pause.

AT A GLANCE

Reflection Type
- Individual response, shared anonymously (use a digital collection app for anonymity)
- Individual response, publicly shared

Delivery Method
- Virtual instructor-led training
- Instructor-led training

Number of Participants
- Any number
- With larger groups, consider using a digital method like Slido or Mentimeter

Time Needed
- 5 minutes or less

Reflection Timing
- During
- After

The Activity

Participants respond with a rating of 1 to 5 to reflect on how useful they find the content you've covered. You can gather responses by asking people to:
- Physically hold up their hands to show one to five fingers.
- Place a number in the chat.
- Use an annotation to stamp the image that fits their feeling.
- Respond to a one-question digital poll.

Step-by-Step Instructions

1. Explain that you are going to check the pulse of the room to gauge everyone's progress.
2. Ask everyone to raise their hands with one finger for low energy, five fingers for high energy, or anywhere in between. (Or choose a similar method.)
3. Demonstrate raising your hand (or dropping a number in the chat or any other method you've chosen).

4. As participants raise their hands, acknowledge the hands you see. Avoid directly asking why if you see low or high numbers.
5. Adjust activities or consider taking a break if you see a lot of low numbers.

Facilitator's Guide

What to Say	What to Do
I'd like to check in with you to see how useful you've found this content so far.	
On a scale of 1 to 5, with 1 being not useful and 5 being extremely useful, show me a number to indicate how you're feeling.	Hold up your hand displaying first 1 finger and then all 5.
You can also share your number in the chat.	Pause.
I'm noticing a range between [note what you see]	Watch the participants to see everyone's numbers.
If numbers are low, ask, "What might make this information more useful for you?"	

How to Increase the Value

- Have you ever pushed a button in a restroom to rate your experience? Typically, you'll see three color-coded buttons (green, yellow, and red). Consider creating a similar easy visual to use for a quick reflection in class.
- Search the internet for "On a scale of. . ." and you'll discover hundreds of well-being scales using images of llamas, cats, sloths, and even pictures of David Bowie! You can use one of these lighthearted scales, or create your own, to help gauge how people are feeling. Consider your participants to determine just how lighthearted you should get!

> **INTERNET EXTRA**
>
> What animal or celebrity would participants respond to best if featured on a 1 to 5 scale? You might even use a leader from your organization (with their permission).

Why I Like This Activity

Of course, I love the rapid-fire response of this activity. Note that inevitably someone will need you to clarify if 1–5 goes most to least or least to most. Be as clear as possible about whether you are channeling a bowling or golf score. (In bowling, you win with a high score; however, the lowest score wins in golf.)

I successfully used On a Scale of 1 to 5 at an in-person conference to gauge everyone's comfort interacting with people they didn't know. The scale was:

- 1 = I am uncomfortable with new people.
- 5 = Bring on the new connections!

Everyone shared their number at the beginning of the session. With each activity, I was able to announce the corresponding number, inviting people to participate or observe based on their comfort level.

Give It a Try

Indicate how you are feeling about what you've read so far using the 5-point face scale. Take a moment to think about what inspired your choice and write it in the space provided.

On a scale of 1 to 5, how you are feeling about what you've read so far?

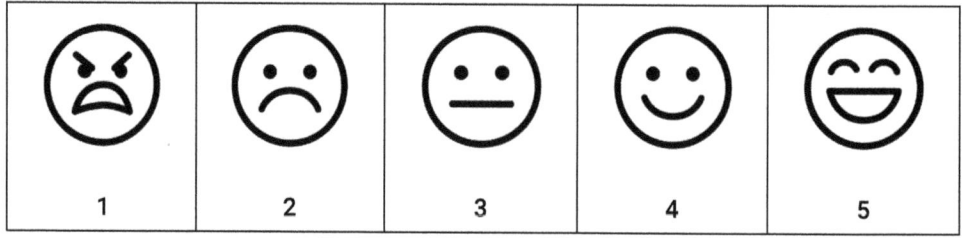

> **NOW ASK YOURSELF**
>
> - When could you use On a Scale of 1 to 5?
> - Whom would this reflection activity work well for?
> - How could you adapt On a Scale of 1 to 5 to fit your training programs?

I Like, I Wish, I Wonder

We are now going to use the idea of wonders once again, along with likes and wishes. In this activity, three short statements give everyone a moment to reflect on their experiences by thinking about what they've enjoyed, what they'd prefer to change, and what else they are curious about.

AT A GLANCE

Reflection Type
- Individual response, private
- Paired response, private
- Small group response, private

Delivery Method
- Virtual instructor-led training
- Instructor-led training

Number of Participants
- Any number

Time Needed
- 5–10 minutes

Reflection Timing
- During
- After

The Activity

We will revisit Instructional Origami with this activity. Provide everyone with an 8.5x11 piece of paper. Ask them to fold it into thirds and label each third with the words "I Like," "I Wish," and "I Wonder." Give them a few minutes to reflect on each column and then ask them to write down their response.

Alternatively, you can create a whiteboard with three columns labeled I Like, I Wish, and I Wonder. Then invite the group to add sticky notes with their ideas to the appropriate columns.

Step-by-Step Instructions

1. Explain that you would like everyone to reflect on their experience in class.
2. Ask everyone to fold a piece of paper into thirds, as if they were folding a letter to put in an envelope.
3. Label the columns I Like, I Wish, and I Wonder.
4. Ask everyone to take a few minutes to reflect on what they like, wish, and wonder about their class experience.

Facilitator's Guide

What to Say	What to Do
We are going to take a few minutes to reflect on our experiences in class.	
Fold your paper in thirds like you are going to mail it in an envelope.	Provide everyone with a piece of paper. Demonstrate the folding pattern.
Please label each column. Write I Like on the first column, I Wish on the second, and I Wonder on the third.	Show an example.
Take a few minutes to reflect on each column.	Consider setting a 5-to-7-minute timer.
Finish the thought you are on.	

How to Increase the Value

- Fold the paper into four columns. The fourth, I Will, helps ground reflection in action.
- Form small groups and ask group members to discuss something they've written in their wonder columns.

Why I Like This Activity

I like the versatility of this activity because it can be used in person or virtually. I've also had a lot of success doing a large group version of this activity at the midpoint of a multipart training course.

This activity also helps me determine in real time what is or is not working for everyone and what questions they might have. It allows me to adjust my plans according to their reflections, and they get the added benefits of additional reflection.

Note, however, that it's not unusual to see people say, "I wish there were more breaks," or "I wish there were snacks."

Give It a Try

Think about what you've read so far in this book about reflection. Use the space provided to list what you like about reflection, what you wish you could change, and what you wonder about reflection.

I Like	I Wish	I Wonder

NOW ASK YOURSELF

- When could you use I Like, I Wish, I Wonder?
- Whom would this reflection method work well for?
- How could you adapt I Like, I Wish, I Wonder to fit your training programs?

Just One Word

Are you short on time but want everyone to have a chance to reflect? In that situation, Just One Word is the perfect activity.

Participants are asked to describe a class, an activity, or a topic with only one word. Why does just one word work? Because it's all about the pause. That small moment we take to think through our experience—a pause we rarely allow ourselves. Thinking about one word can be enough to change the way we leave a learning experience.

AT A GLANCE

Reflection Type
- Individual response, publicly shared

Delivery Method
- Virtual instructor-led training
- Instructor-led training

Number of Participants
- Any number
- Consider using a digital tool with more than 25 people

Time Needed
- 2–5 minutes

Reflection Timing
- During
- After

The Activity

At a natural stopping point in class (the end of a section, before a break, before lunch, or at the end of a session), ask everyone to think of one word to describe their experience. Give them a moment to pause, think, and then share their word with the full group or in small groups.

If you are training virtually, ask everyone to unmute and share, type into the chat, or annotate onto the screen.

Step-by-Step Instructions

1. Tell participants it's time to check in with everyone in the room.
2. Ask everyone to think of just one word to describe their experience so far in class.
3. Wait a short time for everyone to think of their word.
4. Ask them to share their word out loud, in the chat, or to a shared whiteboard space.
5. Ask participants which words stand out and discuss.
6. Highlight a few words that resonate with you

Facilitator's Guide

What to Say	What to Do
Let's take a moment to check in with everyone.	
I'd like you to think of just one word to describe how you are feeling right now.	
Give me a nod or thumbs-up when you have your one word.	Watch for acknowledgment that everyone is ready.
Please share your word.	
What do you notice about everyone's words?	
Do you see any themes in the words?	Take a break or change activities if energy appears low.

How to Increase the Value

- Record the words and compare them with other words chosen during other parts of the learning experience. Ask everyone to share what they notice about the words collected from the beginning to the end of the program.
- Combine Just One Word with Chat Cascade for a quick, effective view of everyone's feelings.

Why I Like This Activity

I use the Just One Word activity to check the pulse of everyone in class—but that's not my only reason.

Don't we all have those moments when we doubt if we are reaching people in our classes? I like the ego boost this check-in can provide when positive words cascade through the chat. Hearing or reading everyone's words offers immediate positive feedback.

On the other hand, less-than-positive responses give me the opportunity to evaluate changes I can make to the training program.

Give It a Try

Can you think of one word to describe your experience of reading this book? Write it in the space provided.

Write down one word to describe your experience of reading this book.

NOW ASK YOURSELF

- When could you use Just One Word?

- Whom would this reflection method work well for?

- How could you adapt this activity to fit people in your training programs?

I'll Use/Tell Me More

I'll Use/Tell Me More is a method of asking people to reflect on what they will use from class when they return to work and what they want to know more about. It's an activity that works well before a break or at the end of the day when doing multiple days of training.

I'll Use/Tell Me More provides reflection for participants and an opportunity for you, the facilitator, to consider what people need more of for a successful learning experience.

AT A GLANCE

Reflection Type
- Individual response, shared anonymously

Delivery Method
- Virtual instructor-led training
- Instructor-led training

Number of Participants
- Any number
- With groups larger than 25, consider using a digital polling tool to help sort responses

Time Needed
- 5–10 minutes

Reflection Timing
- During
- After

The Activity

This can be an extremely low-tech activity. You'll simply provide participants with two sticky notes each. After they reflect on their experiences by writing what ideas or information they will use and what they'd like to know more about, you'll post them to a shared place. No names or identifying information are needed.

While this activity works for both virtual and in person training, the steps differ based on the delivery method.

Step-by-Step Instructions for vILT

1. Let everyone know that they are going to take a moment to reflect on their learning experience.
2. Open a virtual whiteboard with two sticky notes per person.
3. On one sticky note, ask participants to write something they will use from class. On the second sticky note, ask them to write something they want to know more about.

4. Ask them to place their notes in the appropriate column.
5. Invite them to sort the notes into the major themes they notice.
6. Discuss the themes.
7. Ask what issues they notice during the discussion.
8. Provide insight or resources to address the Tell Me More sticky notes.

Facilitator's Guide for vILT

What to Say	What to Do
Before we wrap up, let's take a moment to reflect on your experience so far.	
Grab two sticky notes.	Open a digital whiteboard.
On the first sticky note, type one thing you will use from today.	Provide a visual example.
On the second note, write one thing you'd like to know more about.	Provide a visual example.
Once you've typed yours, place them in their appropriate columns.	
When you return, we'll discuss them.	Discuss the common themes in the notes when everyone returns. Consider providing follow-up information if needed.

Step-by-Step Instructions for ILT

1. Let everyone know they are going to take a moment to reflect on their learning experience.
2. Give everyone two sticky notes. Any color will do!
3. Ask participants to write something they will use from class on the first note. Ask them to write something they want to know more about on the second sticky note.
4. Invite them to place their notes in a shared location as they leave for a break or at the end of a multiday session.
5. Review and sort the notes so you can discuss any major themes when class resumes.
6. Ask what issues they notice during the discussion.
7. Provide insight or resources to address the Tell Me More sticky notes.

Facilitator's Guide for ILT

What to Say	What to Do
Before we wrap up, let's take a moment to reflect on your experience so far.	
Grab two sticky notes.	Provide sticky notes.
On the first sticky note, write one thing you will use from today.	Provide a visual example.
On the second note, write one thing you'd like to know more about.	Provide a visual example.
Once you've written yours, place them in their appropriate columns.	Provide a shared place to display notes.
When you return, we'll discuss them.	Discuss the common themes in the notes when everyone returns. Consider providing follow-up information if needed.

How to Increase the Value

- Place the sticky notes in a prominent location to return to throughout a program.
- Provide resources for the Tell Me More notes after class.
- Ask small groups to discuss ideas from the chart.

Why I Like This Activity

I love using this reflection to help me decide what to discuss in more detail. Tell Me More replaces the typical, "What questions do you have?"

Make sure to give people enough time to reflect, formulate, and post their responses. It's always helpful to provide a few examples. And remember that most people don't want to be the first to answer either question; your examples can help overcome that.

Want faster responses? Do this right before heading to a break as an "exit ticket." The reflection may not be as deep, but the responses will fly in!

(I first used this reflection during an in-person class and called it Flipchart Feedback. The two reflective statements haven't changed, but I altered the name for the virtual training environment.)

Give It a Try

Think about what you've read so far in this book. In the space provided, write down what you'll use and what I can tell you more about.

I'll Use	Tell Me More

NOW ASK YOURSELF

- When could you use I'll Use/Tell Me More?
- Which groups would this reflection approach be most helpful for?
- What changes would make this a perfect fit for your group?

Conclusion

Never forget: Fast reflection is still reflection!

The time we take for a cognitive break, to check in with one another, and to adjust direction when needed is essential. Throughout this chapter, we've explored several quick reflection activities that can assess progress:

- **The Chat Cascade:** Provides a rapid-fire method to gather authentic reflections from all participants simultaneously, encouraging responsiveness and preventing copying
- **On a Scale of 1 to 5:** A simple yet effective way to gauge everyone's energy, understanding, or comfort levels quickly and visually
- **I Like, I Wish, I Wonder:** Allows participants to express appreciation, desire for improvement, and curiosity, providing a comprehensive snapshot of their experience
- **One Word:** An ultra-quick reflection that encourages participants to distill their experience or feelings into a single, potent word
- **I'll Use/Tell Me More:** Helps identify immediate takeaways and areas where participants want more information

Each of these activities serves multiple purposes:

- Provide everyone with a moment to pause and process their experience.
- Offer facilitators valuable insight into the group's energy, understanding, and needs.
- Can help manage cognitive load by providing brief mental breaks.
- Allow for real-time adjustments to content delivery and pacing.

Placing these quick reflective activities strategically throughout a learning experience helps people consider how they are feeling *in the moment*. As a facilitator, you can use this information to adjust content, add explanations, and alter your course to meet the needs of participants.

Remember, the goal isn't just to collect data, but to create a responsive and adaptive learning environment as well. By regularly assessing progress, you're not only improving the immediate learning experience, but also modeling reflective practice—a skill that participants can carry forward into their professional lives.

As you implement these activities, be flexible and responsive. The specific activity you choose is less important than the act of pausing for reflection itself. Experiment with different methods, adapt them to your context, and be ready to respond to the feedback you receive.

FINAL QUESTIONS FOR REFLECTION

Take a moment to think about a learning experience you are designing or delivering. Consider where a pulse check or quick assessment might be beneficial.

Ask yourself:

- How are you currently assessing progress during training?
- Where do you need to add a reflective activity to assess progress?
- Which activities work best for the training program you are designing?

Chapter 8
Outcome 6: Improve Performance

Follow effective action with quiet reflection. From the quiet reflection will come even more effective action.
—Peter Drucker, author and business strategist

When I was a kid and made the mistakes kids make, my parents would say, "Think about what you've done," and send me to my room. It was a common approach to parenting as harsher punishment became less common. At first glance, their method seems like quiet desperation, but they were encouraging me to reflect on my actions. Reflecting on our performance, both when it's good and when it needs improvement, is an important part of the process of behavior change.

Ultimately, my parents discovered that I liked being alone in my room with my books and my journal, away from my four siblings. It took only a moment of reflection on their part to punish me with a seat in the middle of the living room, surrounded by my family.

Better Performance for Organizational Success

Training exists to improve workplace performance. Training can also help develop individuals' personal skills and provide opportunities for growth in many areas, but the organizations we work for and with as L&D professionals exist to fulfill missions. Those missions can serve shareholders, members, or the common good, but in all cases, improving employees' performance on the job is essential to success.

Organizational success relies on many things, and among the most important is the ability to reflect on our own performance. Those of us who take the time to intentionally consider our performance reveal opportunities for our growth and development. Research has shown a powerful link between reflection and performance (Di Stefano et al. 2023). Even a short amount of reflection on our work can improve our performance.

Are you covering difficult content in a training course that requires changing an existing behavior? Always allow for a few minutes of personal reflection before you move to group reflection. These few minutes increase the value of reflection and allow more time for process thinkers to reflect on their experiences.

We all take more responsibility for our performance when we've reflected on both our successes and our failures (Ellis et al. 2006). And after carefully thinking about our performance, we can then create improvements that last.

Activities

The activities in this chapter help participants reflect on their learning and their performance at work to create action plans they can transfer to their jobs. The activities range from simple two-question reflections to more complex reviews.

Insight and Action

Many people who study reflection suggest three to five steps in the ideal reflective process, but sometimes two questions are enough. In this activity, participants will take less than 10 minutes to consider a key insight or idea from class and then outline the steps they will take to implement it. This is particularly useful at the end of a learning module or experience to reinforce learning and encourage immediate application.

AT A GLANCE

Reflection Type
- Individual response, private
- Individual response, publicly shared
- Small group response, private
- Small group response, publicly shared
- Large group response

Delivery Method
- Virtual instructor-led training
- Instructor-led training

Number of Participants
- Any number

Time Needed
- 5–10 minutes

Reflection Timing
- After

The Activity

Everyone reflects on the content or activities they've experienced in training, selecting one specific insight or idea that resonated with them. They will write both their insight and steps for implementing it and share their reflections with a small group or in the large group as time allows.

I often use 3x5 index cards for this activity when in person, but you can also use a digital note-taking tool.

Step-by-Step Instructions

1. Give everyone a 3x5 index card.
2. Ask them to identify a key idea or insight from class on one side of the card.
3. On the other side of the card, have them list the steps they need to take to implement the idea or insight at work.
4. When everyone has completed the exercise, assemble participants in small groups to share their insights and steps for implementation.

Facilitator's Guide

What to Say	What to Do
Grab a 3x5 card. One per person. We are going to do a quick reflection.	Provide 3x5 index cards to everyone (or ask them to use a digital note-taking tool and revise the instructions accordingly).
On one side of the card, list a key idea or insight from the material we've just completed.	Show an example, specifically focusing on the learning objective or activity you want participants to reflect on. Wait until everyone appears to be ready.
Now, flip your card over, and on the other side, write the steps you can take to implement your idea or insight.	Show an example. Wait 3 to 5 minutes or until everyone appears ready.
Option 1, Pairs • With your partner, please share your insight and actions.	Form pairs.
Option 2, Small Group • In your small group, please share your insights and actions. • Watch your time so everyone has an opportunity to share.	Form small groups of 3–4 people each.
Option 3, Large Group • Let's talk about the insights you wrote down. Who would like to share? • What are the actions you are going to take?	Ask several people to share their insights and actions. If you have access to a tool such as Slido or Mentimeter, you can gather the group's insights, and then discuss the actions.

How to Increase the Value
- Repeat the activity throughout a program for each learning objective.
- For team-based training, consider expanding the activity to cover key insights and steps for the entire team to implement. A team-based activity will require more time.

Why I Like This Activity

I created this activity when I had unexpected extra time during a class. It worked so well that it quickly became a regular part of my repertoire even before I understood the value of reflection.

I love real-life, tactile office supplies of all kinds, so I welcome any opportunity to use index cards, sticky notes, and Mr. Sketch markers. (What facilitator doesn't?) I originally called this activity 3x5 Reflection. Then, I solicited opinions from friends on LinkedIn, who said Insight and Action was more participant focused. And, of course, with our great migration to virtual training in 2020, I wanted to make sure the activity was accessible to everyone, so any form of note-taking—cards, digital, or audio—will work.

Give It a Try

Consider what you've read in this book so far or something you learned from a recent webinar or in-person training. Write down one insight or idea in the space provided. Then, list the steps you'll take to implement the idea.

Insight	Steps to Implement

NOW ASK YOURSELF

- When could you use Insight and Action?
- Whom would this reflection method work well for?
- How could you adapt this activity to fit your training programs?

Start, Stop, Continue

Start, Stop, Continue is based on the classic feedback method Stop, Keep, Start (SKS) created by Phil Daniels, a psychology professor at Brigham Young University. I've altered SKS to focus on performance reflection, asking participants to reflect on what they can start, stop, and continue after a learning experience. It provides a simple framework that mirrors our natural tendency to reflect on what has worked and what has not.

It's best to conduct this activity at the end of a program as an action plan that you or participants' managers can use to check in on the extent of learning transfer to the job.

AT A GLANCE

Reflection Type
- Individual response, private
- Individual response, publicly shared
- Paired response, private
- Paired response, publicly shared
- Small group response, private
- Small group response, publicly shared
- Large group response

Delivery Method
- Virtual instructor-led training
- Instructor-led training

Number of Participants
- Any number

Time Needed
- 5–15 minutes

Reflection Timing
- After

The Activity

All participants are asked to consider what they will start, stop, and continue doing based on the content of a course or module. They will reflect and write multiple items under each category if possible. In pairs or small groups, everyone then shares their answers.

Step-by-Step Instructions

1. Ask everyone to draw and label (Start, Stop, Continue) three columns on a sheet of paper or digital document. Alternatively, provide a prepared document for each participant, with three columns.
2. Ask participants to reflect on their experience in the course or module, identifying what they intend to start, stop, and continue going forward. Encourage the use of active verbs to make after-class actions easier to identify.

3. When everyone is done making notes (approximately five to 15 minutes), ask them to discuss in pairs, small groups, or the large group.

Facilitator's Guide

What to Say	What to Do
We are going to take a few minutes to reflect on what you would like to start, stop, and continue doing after today's experience.	Provide everyone with a prepared paper or digital document, or a blank piece of paper.
Take the next five minutes to write a list of what you'd like to start, stop, and continue. You'll be sharing this in pairs [*or small groups or our large group*] when you are done.	Set a quiet 5-minute timer. Adjust the time for deeper reflection. Adjust your statement for pairs, small groups, or the large group.
Option 1, Pairs • With your partner, please discuss what you are going to start, stop, and continue.	Form pairs.
Option 2, Small Group • In your small group, please discuss what you are going to start, stop, and continue. • Watch your time so everyone has an opportunity to share.	Form small groups of 3–4 people each.
Option 3, Large Group • Let's talk about what you are going to stop, start, and continue. • Let's begin with start.	Ask several people to share from their lists. Alternatively, use Slido or Mentimeter to collect the information.

How to Increase the Value

- Use an Instructional Origami approach, asking each participant to fold a piece of paper into three parts and label the three columns "Start," "Stop," and "Continue."
- Consider beginning a learning experience with this reflection, asking people to return to it from time to time and inviting them to use it when they identify something new they want to start, stop, or continue.
- Add a fourth column, Change, to the activity to capture specific changes participants might make.
- Try using Trainers Warehouse's "Start, Stop, Continue, Change" sticky notes to gather reflection throughout your learning experience.

Why I Like This Activity

Start, Stop, Continue is one of the easiest activities for everyone to understand. The three simple questions provide a framework that works for participants regardless of their role.

You may have encountered it before and consider it old school. But I've found it works well, so I prefer to think of it as a classic. When people get to the question of what they will continue, it helps them acknowledge that they are already doing some things well, an important motivational support.

Give It a Try

Consider what you will start, stop, and continue as a result of reading this book and list at least two items in each column.

Start	Stop	Continue

NOW ASK YOURSELF

- When could you use Start, Stop, Continue?
- What groups would this reflection method work well for?
- How could you adapt this activity to fit your training programs?

It's a RAP (Reflection Action Plan)

Planning is a way of reflecting on the future, drawing upon our past experiences to move forward. Action planning requires us to consider where we want to go given everything we've experienced.

The action-planning format I'm suggesting here asks participants to consider what they have learned in a particular training course and how it can be applied to the workplace. This method takes longer than many other activities and is best suited for multiday, complex learning experiences.

AT A GLANCE

Reflection Type
- Individual response, private

Delivery Method
- Virtual instructor-led training
- Instructor-led training
- E-learning
- Self-directed learning

Number of Participants
- Any number

Time Needed
- 10–20 minutes

Reflection Timing
- After

The Activity

Everyone considers three key things they've learned and how those three things relate to their work. Based on what they've learned, they then identify actions they will take and create a timeline for the actions. They also identify potential problems they might encounter and methods to minimize those issues. Finally, they outline a plan to check their progress.

Step-by-Step Instructions

1. Let everyone know they will be taking part in an action-planning reflection. Consider setting an expectation at the beginning of the program that they will be asked to reflect on later.
2. Provide the action-planning template.
3. Provide time for everyone to complete the template.
4. Discussion of individual action plans is optional but encouraged.

Facilitator's Guide

What to Say	What to Do
Reflecting on your performance helps you remember information and transfer what you've learned here into the workplace. Reflection can be essential for your success.	
You are invited to complete an action plan to help you identify three actions to take after class, along with steps to help you analyze each action.	Show an example. The detail of the example will depend on the needs of your participants. (See appendix B for an example of what to provide.)
You'll have the next 15 minutes to begin your action plan. You may not finish today, and I encourage you to continue working on the plan after class.	Set a quiet timer for 15 minutes.
Go ahead and finish the thought you are on. Thank you for taking time to reflect.	

How to Increase the Value

- At the end of the activity, add extra time for participants to share their plans in small groups and compare and discuss.
- Use a debrief activity like What? Gut? So What? Now What? to reflect on the process.
- Ask participants how you can help support their progress after today.
- If participants are learning with their full team, consider completing the action plan together. Begin with individual reflection on the three actions, and then facilitate a conversation about the top team priorities.

Why I Like This Activity

Extended reflection time can lead to deeper thinking and increase benefits from the process.

Planning our actions increases our likelihood of success. While we often try to keep reflections short and add elements of fun, the action-planning process takes reflection more seriously and provides more time than most activities.

I've found It's a RAP is most successful with people in technical fields, including engineers and scientists. They often include specific requests for me to connect with them after a training experience.

Give It a Try

Consider what you've read in this book so far to complete the action plan provided. You may want to bookmark this page and return to it later.

Reflect

What are three important things you learned in [program name]?
1.
2.
3.

How do these three things relate to your work?
1.
2.
3.

Plan

When you return to work, what action(s) will you take based on items 1-3 above?
1.
2.
3.

By When?
1.
2.
3.

What support will you need?

Possible Obstacles

What will make it difficult to accomplish your plan?

How can you minimize these obstacles?

Checking Progress

What will you measure to check the progress of your plan?

How can *[name]* help support your progress after today?

NOW ASK YOURSELF

- When could you use It's a RAP?
- What groups would this reflection method work well for?
- How could you adapt this activity to fit your training programs?

Pause, Breathe, Think

Time is all you need for reflection. The Pause, Breathe, Think activity asks everyone to do just what the title says. Providing participants with a concept or piece of content to focus on can be helpful for those more reluctant to reflect. You can also use this reflection to help increase performance or include it in training when you need a quick reset of the group's energy and focus. Adding it to the beginning of a training experience can help people set aside other distractions and be present.

AT A GLANCE

Reflection Type
- Individual response, private
- Individual response, publicly shared
- Large group response

Delivery Method
- Virtual instructor-led training
- Instructor-led training
- E-learning
- Self-directed learning

Number of Participants
- Any number

Time Needed
- 2–5 minutes

Reflection Timing
- Before
- During
- After

The Activity

This activity is one of the simplest—no gimmicks or tricks involved! And no writing! Everyone pauses, takes a deep breath, and thinks about something specific from their learning experience. I like to encourage participants to think about an idea that they will implement when they return to work.

Step-by-Step Instructions

1. Ask everyone to sit comfortably.
2. Ask them to stop anything they are doing, including glancing at computer screens, notebooks, or phones. Invite them to pause.
3. Ask them to close their eyes if that is comfortable for them.
4. Ask them to take a deep breath.
5. Demonstrate the deep breath.

6. Ask them to think about the value of what they've learned.
7. Ask them to open their eyes.
8. Thank them for taking a moment to reflect.

Facilitator's Guide

What to Say	What to Do
We are going to take a moment to reflect on what you've learned so far.	
Please pause with me for a moment, setting aside anything you're doing or looking at.	
Close your eyes if that is comfortable for you.	
Now take a deep breath. Breathe in, hold it, and let it go.	Demonstrate a deep breath.
Now take a few minutes to think about the value of what we've covered so far.	Remain quiet. Consider playing soft, wordless music.

How to Increase the Value

- Add a few minutes of discussion at the end of the activity, letting volunteers share their thoughts.
- Walk everyone through a longer breathing exercise before you ask them to think. It could go like this:
  - Place your feet on the ground.
  - Drop your chin to your chest.
  - Relax your shoulders.
  - Take a breath in and out.
  - Sit up straight.
  - Take a deep breath in.
  - Let it go.

Why I Like This Activity

Don't underestimate things you can't see. Attention and reflection happen in our brains, so we don't always have to put the results down on paper. In *The Art and Science of Training*, Elaine Biech (2016) refers to reflection as "invisible learning."

So now, put your feet on the ground and take a moment to pause, breathe, and think about when you could use Pause, Breathe, Think in your work.

Give It a Try

Pause, take a deep breath, and think about one specific thing you've learned in this chapter or from a recent discussion of L&D with a colleague.

NOW ASK YOURSELF

- When could you use Pause, Breathe, Think?
- What groups would this reflection method work well for?
- How could you adapt this activity to fit your training program?

Just Imagine

Using our imaginations to conjure mental images—especially if we visualize success—can improve our performance. For example, athletes often benefit from visualization in both their performance and their psychological well-being (Jose and Joseph 2018). Visualization techniques can diminish anxiety and boost self-confidence in phenomenal ways.

If we add movement to our mental images, we see even more benefits. My son, an avid Dungeons & Dragons Dungeon Master, has spent time bouncing on an exercise ball imagining the campaigns he's going to lead. He finds that the combination of exercise and reflection helps him work out intricate scenarios and plan his responses to challenges.

AT A GLANCE

Reflection Type
- Individual response, private
- Individual response, publicly shared

Delivery Method
- Virtual instructor-led training
- Instructor-led training
- E-learning
- Self-directed learning

Number of Participants
- Any number

Time Needed
- 3–7 minutes

Reflection Timing
- During
- After

The Activity

Participants will be asked to find a comfortable position and imagine themselves performing a task they've practiced in the current training course. They'll be asked what they see; how they feel; and what they might be touching, hearing, smelling, or tasting (if taste is relevant).

Pause for at least three minutes to give them quiet time to just imagine. (Note that sharing thoughts after reflecting is optional.)

Step-by-Step Instructions

1. Invite everyone to find a comfortable position.
2. If participants are learning virtually, request that they turn their cameras off.
3. Ask them to imagine themselves performing a task covered in the current training course, such as providing feedback, operating machinery, or making a sales call.

4. Ask:
   - What do you see?
   - How do you feel?
   - What are you touching or holding?
   - What do you hear?
   - What do you smell?
   - What do you taste?
5. Provide three to seven minutes for them to imagine.
6. Thank them for their time, explaining that visualization is a powerful tool to help increase confidence and reduce anxiety.

Facilitator's Guide

What to Say	What to Do
Professional athletes use mental imagery to practice and improve. Research shows that this improves confidence and performance. I'm going to invite you to imagine your own performance.	
Find a comfortable position. [If learning virtually] Turn off your cameras.	
Close your eyes if that is comfortable for you.	
Now imagine yourself performing this specific task: [Identify the task].	
Think about what you see and what you feel. Think about what you hear and what you are holding or touching. Think about what you smell and what you taste. We're going to pause now so you can imagine the scenario fully.	Pause for 3 to 7 minutes. Wait quietly.
Please open your eyes if you closed them. Thank you for taking time to imagine your performance.	

How to Increase the Value

- Consider adding movement to this activity. Invite everyone to go for a short walk inside or outside while imagining.
- Follow this activity with a debrief of the experience, asking participants to share what they saw and felt.

Why I Like This Activity

Did you know that 1 to 4 percent of people live with aphantasia, or the inability to form visual images when thinking? I considered not including this activity for that reason.

But, as someone with a vivid imagination, it's hard for me to eliminate that from the way I process information, including reflection. I decided to include this activity because research supports mental imaging as a powerful tool for reflection and learning transfer. In addition to athletes, professional speakers, actors, and others use this technique to help them reflect on and practice their performance.

Give It a Try

Read the following statement, and then take a moment to use your imagination as described.

> Imagine yourself leading a reflection activity during an upcoming learning experience you've been planning:
>
> - What do you see in the room around you?
> - How does it feel?
> - What are you touching?
> - What sounds do you hear?
> - What do you smell?

NOW ASK YOURSELF

- When could you use Just Imagine?
- What groups would this reflection method work well for?
- How could you adapt this activity to fit your training programs?

After-Action Review

The after-action review is a team-based activity that helps develop a shared view of an experience and a shared path forward. By delving deeply into what happened in a learning experience and why, we are able to build a foundation for behavior change.

In this activity, I am repurposing the after-action review to be used individually or as a team. I've found it's beneficial to use this activity four to five weeks after the conclusion of a learning experience, as people are in the process of transferring learning to the workplace.

While After-Action Review can be used with individuals or groups, note that advanced facilitation skills are required for facilitating group reflection.

AT A GLANCE

Reflection Type
- Individual response, private
- Large group response

Delivery Method
- Virtual instructor-led training
- Instructor-led training

Number of Participants
- 2–25

Time Needed
- 15 minutes for individuals
- 30–60 minutes for groups

Reflection Timing
- After

The Activity

You'll lead a group of participants methodically through a series of questions asking about their learning experience.

Participants will explore four key questions individually or as a group:
- What did you expect to happen?
- What happened?
- Why was there a difference between what you expected and what happened?
- Moving forward, what actions can you take?

Through discussion and group reflection, participants build a shared view of what happened, why reality didn't meet expectations, and actions that should change in the future.

Step-by-Step Instructions for Individual Reflection
1. Let everyone know they are going to reflect on their learning experience.
2. Provide an After-Action Review template.
3. Explain the four key questions:
   - What did you expect to happen?
   - What happened?
   - Why was there a difference between what you expected and what happened?
   - Moving forward, what actions can you take?
4. Suggest they spend the most time on the second question.
5. Provide time to complete the after-action review.

Facilitator's Guide

What to Say	What to Do
Reflecting on your experience is essential for both your long-term retention and performance on the job.	
I'm going to provide you with an after action review template. This format is often used to debrief teams after projects are completed to determine what changes should be made moving forward.	Provide a template. Consider sharing a completed example (such as the one provided in appendix B).
Take the next 15 minutes to respond to the four questions. Spend most of your time on the second question, diving deep into what happened during your learning experience.	Provide a silent 15 minutes to complete the after action review.
Please finish the thought you are on. If you need to continue after class, please do.	

Step-by-Step Instructions for Group Reflection
1. Tell the group they are going to reflect on their shared learning experience.
2. Ask them to consider what they expected to happen.
3. Discuss what actually happened. Spend the bulk of the time on what happened to create a shared view.
4. Once a shared view of what happened is reached, move to the next question.
5. Ask everyone why there was a difference between expectations.
6. Finally, discuss changes to make moving forward.

Facilitator's Guide

What to Say	What to Do
Reflecting on our shared experience is essential for both long-term retention and performance changes on the job.	
Let's discuss the expectations you started with.	Lead a discussion on the expectations everyone started with. Encourage everyone to share their expectations. Consider using Mentimeter or Slido to gather participants' thoughts in a large group.
Now, most important, let's discuss what actually happened.	Lead a discussion, hearing from everyone and validating personal experiences. Work to create a shared view of experiences.
With our shared view in mind, let's continue to our final questions.	
Why was there a difference between what we expected and what happened?	Discuss, documenting key points.
Moving forward, what actions can we take in the future?	Finish the discussion with a focus on next actions, documenting the group's agreed upon actions.
Thank you for taking the time to help review our experience.	

How to Increase the Value

- Consider conducting this a month after a learning experience to focus on the change in behaviors and the value of the experience.
- Ask everyone to answer the expectation questions at the beginning of a learning experience for a more precise view of expectations.
- Add a final step to the individual reflection inviting everyone to share the actions they want to take next.

Why I Like This Activity

If you are working with people who are skeptical of reflection, After-Action Review can be a great alternative because they will likely see it as practical.

Developed by the US Army, the after-action review has been used successfully in almost every profession and economic sector and in a variety of situations. The key is encouraging people to focus deeply on the second question and creating a complete view of what happened before moving forward to next actions.

Give It a Try

Consider what you've read in this book so far or another recent learning experience as you answer the following questions. The questionnaire should take 15 minutes to complete, and you'll want to spend the most time on the second question. Consider saving this for after you've finished reading the entire book.

---

1. What did you expect to happen?

2. What actually happened?

3. Why was there a difference between what was expected and what happened?

4. What can you change next time?

NOW ASK YOURSELF

- What did you like about After-Action Review?
- When could you use After-Action Review?
- What groups would this reflection method work well for?
- How could you adapt this activity to fit your learning experiences?

Conclusion

I grew up playing the arcade game Centipede. Arcade etiquette dictated that you should place a quarter on the game to claim the next play. I remember scooting my coin into the corner of the game and eagerly waiting for my turn at the trackball.

I recently found the original game at an arcade and quickly dropped my tokens in to relive the joy. Over the previous 20 years or so, I'd had some time to reflect on the game. After three tragic deaths in the game, I was delighted to see I had a chance to add my name to the list of top scores. I think I was playing better than I had ever played because reflection led me to see the game and my strategy differently. I'd had time to process and think about it, even though I hadn't played in years.

Reflection improves our performance. It helps us think about what we've done and identify what we could do differently in the future. Whether it's arcade games or work tasks, we *need* reflection for improved performance.

In this chapter, you explored activities to help improve performance:

- **Insight and Action:** A reflection to identify a key insight and outline steps to implement it
- **Start, Stop, Continue:** A quick reflection on what people will start, stop, and continue doing after the learning experience
- **It's a RAP:** A detailed action plan that identifies three key takeaways and how to apply them
- **Pause, Breathe, Think:** A quick reflection in which participants pause, take a deep breath, and think about what they've learned
- **Just Imagine:** A way to use mental imagery to visualize successfully performing a task covered in training
- **After-Action Review:** A structured reflection process examining expectations, actual events, reasons for differences, and future actions

Taking time for reflection helps people gain new perspectives and connect their new experiences to their previous experiences, ultimately providing more durable learning. When our learning lasts, we are more likely to change our performance on the job.

FINAL QUESTIONS FOR REFLECTION

Think of a learning experience you anticipate designing or delivering soon and reflect on how reflection might be beneficial for improved performance.

Ask yourself:

- When have you noticed reflection improve performance?

- Which of your learning experiences would benefit from a few activities designed to improve performance?

- Which activities in this chapter fit your programs best?

- What modifications could you make to any of the activities for a better fit for your topic or participants?

Chapter 9
Outcome 7: Sharpen Critical Thinking

Critical thinking requires us to use our imagination, seeing things from perspectives other than our own and envisioning the likely consequences of our position.
—bell hooks, American author and social activist

For quite a while, I've been obsessed with the band Mumford & Sons. Seriously, obsessed. I've listened to their album *Sigh No More* on repeat during more than one cross-country flight. When I arrive home, it continues to play on repeat in my head and on my phone. In fact, I'm listening to it as I write these words.

What does this have to do with critical thinking or reflection?

Everything.

Take, for example, the words of one song: "You must know life to see decay." As I listen to the lyrics, I ask, "What does that mean?" In fact, I often pause their music, look up the lyrics, and try to make sense of what I've heard. The music is good, but the lyrics are outstanding and spark my critical thinking. I find myself asking multiple questions to understand the music, the artists, and the influences driving both. I want to know the what, the why, and the how.

Questioning Our Thinking Through Reflection

Engaging our critical thinking allows us to consider our own thinking as well as the intent and meaning of the information we are learning. As critical thinkers, we are paying attention to what's happening in our brains as we take in new information. To sharpen our critical skills, we reflect on our process. We question the information we're receiving and why we believe it or don't. We question how we can use the information.

Today, with answers, essays, and knowledge in every language at our fingertips—just an AI prompt or Google search away—we risk losing our critical-thinking skills. We've seen countless articles, books, and podcasts decry the loss of focus and attention spans in our era of perpetual scrolling. As trainers, we focus on reflection to sharpen critical thinking and to encourage people to ask, "What does that mean?" and "Why did someone make that choice?" Our goal is to lead participants toward asking more critical questions, analyzing information in new ways, and drawing their own conclusions.

While we strive for ideal training situations, we often face requests to deliver content that is better suited for other formats. If your program resembles an information dump more than an opportunity to practice new behaviors or skills, it's essential to add reflection activities that require critical thinking. These activities will create a meaningful connection between the information you share and their workplace application.

Questions for Designers and Facilitators

Think of a learning experience you anticipate designing or delivering soon.
- Who are the participants?
- How skilled are they at critical thinking?
- Where do you need to help increase their critical thinking?

FACILITATING REFLECTION IN ACTION

We aren't always prepared with the perfect activity. You can use the following questions if you want to add quick reflection to a learning experience. They can help participants reevaluate their perspectives and experiences:

- Why does this matter?
- Can you give me an example?
- What's another way to look at this issue?
- How do you know this?

Activities

I judge my life events—including gathering with friends, facilitating training, gardening, watching movies, reading books, and traveling—based on the quality of my morning-after thoughts. If I wake up without thinking about an event, I know it was not a very valuable or meaningful time. When I wake up reflecting on what happened the day before, I know I've had a high-quality experience worth replicating.

And yes, I often wake up with Mumford & Sons lyrics in my head! Of course, that could be a result of hitting replay too many times.

The activities in this chapter will help people sharpen their critical-thinking skills and improve their learning experiences. The goal should be to ensure that everyone is waking up reflecting on those experiences the morning after.

Five Questions

I love building a solid structure to help people think critically about what they've learned. Five quick, journalistic-style questions can help anyone frame and organize new information. This five-question format is easy to follow in almost any type of learning experience. Answering multiple questions helps participants consider knowledge from different perspectives, which is an essential component of critical thinking.

AT A GLANCE

Reflection Type
- Individual response, private
- Individual response, publicly shared
- Paired response, private
- Paired response, publicly shared
- Small group response, private
- Small group response, publicly shared
- Large group response

Delivery Method
- Virtual instructor-led training
- Instructor-led training
- E-learning
- Self-directed learning

Number of Participants
- Any number

Time Needed
- 15–20 minutes

Reflection Timing
- After

The Activity

You'll provide individuals or groups with five questions, and they can either write or discuss their answers.

Use this basic structure to frame five questions about your topic:
- **What** have you learned about [*your topic*]?
- **When** will you use what you've learned?
- **Where** will you use what you've learned?
- **How** will you use what you've learned?
- **Why** will you use what you've learned?

The questions build from easier observations to more difficult analysis and focus directly on transfer of learning to the workplace.

Step-by-Step Instructions for Individuals

1. Let everyone know they are going to individually reflect on five questions to help identify what they've learned, and when, where, how, and why they will use it.
2. Provide everyone with a handout with the questions. Alternatively, post the questions where everyone can view them.
3. Provide time to answer the questions.
4. When time is up, invite everyone to share a few of their responses.

Facilitator's Guide

What to Say	What to Do
We are going to take some time to reflect on your experience today.	
I'll give you five questions to reflect on. You can write your responses down. These are for you. Sharing will be optional when you are finished.	Provide a template with the five questions or post them where everyone can view them.
Let me know if you need any clarification as you are working.	
I'll set a 15-minute timer and check in with you when time is up.	Monitor the group, clarifying if needed.

Step-by-Step Instructions for a Group

1. Let everyone know they are going to individually reflect on five questions to help identify what they've learned, and when, where, how, and why they will use it.
2. Provide everyone with a handout with the questions or post the five questions where everyone can view them.
3. Form small groups of three to five people.
4. Set a 15-minute timer.
5. Monitor the groups, clarifying any questions.
6. At the end of 15 minutes, check in with the groups to provide more time if necessary.
7. Conclude with a short debrief of the activity.

Facilitator's Guide

What to Say	What to Do
We are going to take some time to work in groups and reflect on your experience today.	Divide the larger group into smaller groups of 3 to 5 people
I'll give your group five questions to reflect on. You can write your responses down.	Provide a template with the five questions or post them where everyone can view them.
Let me know if you need any clarification as you are working.	
I'll set a 15-minute timer and check in with you when time is up.	Set the timer, monitor the groups, and clarify if needed.
Time's up. Has everyone finished?	Provide more time if required and available.
Let's take a moment to discuss what you wrote down. What stood out for you from your responses?	Provide a debrief of the activity as time allows.

How to Increase the Value

- Five Questions works well as an individual activity but can have rich application with a group. Ask small groups to identify multiple responses to each of the questions.
- After training, send a reminder to participants to review the Five Questions. Encourage discussions with their managers.
- Consider asking managers to discuss employees' responses to the *how* question.
- Use an online polling tool or a shared document to collect and discuss responses.

Why I Like This Activity

Many people benefit from the familiar format of these five questions, making reflection easier. The variety of questions helps people evaluate learning experiences from different viewpoints, leading to more critical analysis and more lasting learning.

My favorite question is the *why* question. It comes last and helps people understand the need for the *how* they've already identified. This is one of the few activities in this book that uses the question *why*. Can you recall why?

Give It a Try

Answer the following five questions for yourself, focusing on what you've read in this book.

Five Questions About Reflection

- What have you learned about reflection in this book?

- When will you use reflection next?

- Where will you practice your own reflection?

- How will you practice reflection?

- Why will you practice reflection?

NOW ASK YOURSELF

- When could you use Five Questions?
- Which groups would this work well for?
- How could you adapt this activity to fit the participants in your training programs?

Plan, Monitor, and Evaluate

Metacognition is often described with the three steps of planning, monitoring, and evaluating. We'll use those three steps to reflect before, during, and after a learning experience. We'll plan for what we want to learn, monitor the plan as we move through a learning experience, and then evaluate our outcomes. Multi-level reflection like this helps people see their learning process more objectively, providing an opportunity to think more critically about their thinking. This is metacognition in action!

This format also helps people become more intentional about what they want out of a learning experience. By repeatedly checking in with what they had planned, they can monitor their progress and establish a more critical view of what they are learning.

AT A GLANCE

Reflection Type
- Individual response, private
- Individual response, publicly shared

Delivery Method
- Virtual instructor-led training
- Instructor-led training
- E-learning
- Self-directed learning

Number of Participants
- Any number

Time Needed
- 3–5 minutes repeated at least 3 times during a learning experience

Reflection Timing
- Before
- During
- After

The Activity

At the beginning of a training program, you'll ask everyone to identify what they plan to learn. Consider providing a list of learning objectives or a course outline to help them get started.

Throughout the program, you'll invite participants to look at their plans again, adding what they've learned. At the end of the program, ask everyone to identify how they will use what they've learned. This will become a checklist or a written record of what they've learned.

Step-by-Step Instructions
1. Explain the benefit of reflecting before, during, and after a learning experience.
2. Provide everyone with the Plan, Monitor, and Evaluate template.
3. Provide the learning experience objectives.
4. Allow three to five minutes for everyone to complete the Plan column.
5. Later in the program, ask everyone to review the Monitor column.
6. At the conclusion of the program, ask everyone to complete the Evaluate column.
7. Ask participants to share a few examples of how they'll use what they've learned.

Facilitator's Guide

What to Say	What to Do
I want you to get the most benefit from your learning experience. One way you can do that is by thinking about what you plan to learn, monitoring what you do learn, and evaluating how you will use what you've learned at work.	
I'm going to provide you each with a Plan, Monitor, and Evaluate template and the learning objectives for our program.	Provide the template and objectives.
Take a moment to check all the objectives you want to learn in this program. Add any additional objectives that aren't listed.	Wait 5 minutes or until everyone indicates they are ready.
We'll come back to this document throughout our program. Feel free to add to the Monitor and Evaluate columns.	Provide time during the program and at the conclusion to complete the Monitor and Evaluate columns.
I'd love to hear a few examples of how you'll use what you've learned.	

How to Increase the Value
- Add short, small group discussions at the end of the activity for people to share their plans.
- Provide a list of the learning points for a program as a checklist with a column labeled *What I've Learned and How I'll Use What I've Learned.*
- Consider using your learning management system to track progress over time.
- Encourage follow-up with managers after the learning program.

Why I Like This Activity

I love directly using the three steps of metacognition throughout a training program. Repeated reflection provides a richer experience and helps create a stronger reflection habit.

While I was working with a group of subject matter experts, they filled in the columns throughout our multiple weeks together. At the end of class, they compared each other's work, evaluating the information they'd written and the drawings they'd added to each column. Those with more drawings jokingly asked me for extra credit! I did not intend to gamify reflection, but might encourage it in the future!

Give It a Try

Consider what you plan to learn, what you've already learned, and how you'll use your learning about reflection as a result of reading this book. Note your thoughts in the space provided.

Plan: What I Plan to Learn	Monitor: What I've Learned	Evaluate: How I'll Use What I've Learned

NOW ASK YOURSELF

- When could you use Plan, Monitor, and Evaluate?
- Which group of participants would this work well for?
- How could you adapt this activity to fit your training program?

What Went Well? What Could Be Better?

What went well? What could be better? (Also known in my training classes as WWW-WCBB.) These are two short questions we often ask in our everyday lives that can also help us reflect on learning experiences. We reduce multipart reflection frameworks to the two most essential questions: What happened? And how should we act on what happened?

These two questions can help participants in a training course clarify and celebrate what went well and anticipate ways to improve the experience. They lead us to use critical thinking to plan our actions beyond the end of the learning experience.

AT A GLANCE

Reflection Type
- Individual response, private
- Paired response, private
- Small group response, private
- Large group response

Delivery Method
- Virtual instructor-led training
- Instructor-led training
- E-learning
- Self-directed learning

Number of Participants
- Any number

Time Needed
- 5–10 minutes

Reflection Timing
- After

The Activity

This one is quite simple. You'll provide everyone with the two questions, adjusted to fit the program you're facilitating.

Invite participants to take some time to write their responses. Encourage them to answer honestly and as specifically as possible. Explain that sharing responses is optional, not required.

Step-by-Step Instructions

1. Explain that they are going to take a few minutes to reflect on what they've accomplished in order to translate it into action.
2. Display the two questions, revised to reflect the specifics of your training content.
3. Emphasize that they are considering their learning experience, not the delivery methods used.

4. Ask everyone to write down their responses, making it clear that sharing them is optional, not required.
5. When everyone has completed their responses, invite anyone who wants to share to do so.
6. If time allows, debrief by asking:
   - What did you notice as you reflected?
   - What was the value of the reflection for you?

Facilitator's Guide

What to Say	What to Do
We are going to take some time to reflect on our shared learning experience.	
Your responses are private. You can share if you are comfortable, but you won't be required to.	
Take a few minutes to respond to two questions: • What went well for you? • What could be better for the future?	Display the two questions. Monitor time and provide any clarifications needed.
Please wrap up the thought you are on. Thank you for taking time to reflect.	
[If time permits, debrief with these questions] • What did you notice as you reflected? • What was the value of this reflection for you?	Lead a debrief as time permits.

How to Increase the Value

- Consider adding small breakout groups of three to four people to discuss the answers to gain a group perspective.
  - For virtual sessions, assign breakout rooms.
  - For in-person training, use stickers or playing cards to designate group membership and meeting locations.
- Take time for WWW-WCBB after each learning objective.
- Ask these questions a few weeks after the conclusion of your training course to refresh ideas and encourage retrieval and reflection.

Why I Like This Activity

What's not to like about reflection with just two questions? This activity is specific and quick, and gets everyone thinking creatively about what could be better.

I've found that getting participants to think about their *experience* and not the *delivery methods* can be the tricky part of this activity. More than once I've had to redirect a group when they begin to compliment the structure of an activity rather than their experience with the activity.

Consider asking everyone to focus on their learning experience, not the facilitator's approach.

Give It a Try

Consider the two questions as they relate to reading this book or to another learning experience you've had recently. Use the space provided to write down your thoughts.

---

1. What went well for you?

2. What could be better?

NOW ASK YOURSELF

- When could you use WWW-WCBB?
- Which participants would this work well for?
- How would you adapt the two questions to fit your training programs?
- How can you plan to follow up after a learning experience?

If/Then

Thinking about the consequences of our actions is a hallmark of critical thinking. And everything has consequences.

What happens when we make one choice over another? *If I do this, what other events and people am I affecting?* What is the outcome of my choices? The If/Then activity helps us think critically about the results that taking one action can create. For example:

- If I finish reading this book, then I can implement the activities.
- If I write down my reflection, then I can review it later.
- If I use reflection activities, then people will be more likely to transfer learning to the workplace!

AT A GLANCE

Reflection Type
- Individual response, private
- Paired response, private
- Small group response, private
- Large group response

Delivery Method
- Virtual instructor-led training
- Instructor-led training
- E-learning
- Self-directed learning

Number of Participants
- Any number

Time Needed
- 3–5 minutes for individual reflection
- 10–15 minutes for group reflection

Reflection Timing
- Before
- During
- After

The Activity

You will ask participants in your program to consider the portion of the learning experience they have just completed. You'll invite them to complete an If/Then phrase based on something they've learned to do in the program. You'll ask them to be as specific as possible. Consider providing a few examples to get started.

Step-by-Step Instructions

1. Let everyone know they are going to take a few minutes to reflect on what they've learned and how it will affect their work.
2. Ask them to help you list the key takeaways from class.
3. Ask them to select a few key takeaways to write in the If/Then format.
4. Provide a few examples, such as:
   - If I leave the car's gas tank empty, then my significant other might go to the gas station to fill it up.

- If I take breaks, then I'll be more productive and avoid burning out.
- If I document my team's processes more succinctly, then it will be easier to onboard new team members consistently.

5. Invite them to take the next five minutes to write their own If/Then statements.
6. When everyone has finished, invite several people to share their statements.

Facilitator's Guide

What to Say	What to Do
We are going to take a few minutes to reflect on what you've experienced so far.	
Now, help me out. I've got an If/Then statement, and I'd like you to help me fill in the then. We'll do one together, and then you'll do several on your own.	
This is an effective way to think critically about what you are experiencing. It helps you make the abstract a bit more practical.	
Here's our first example: If we take time for reflection, then we will create more durable learning.	Display your example.
Now let's work on one together: If _____, then _____. How will you fill in the blanks?	Provide a few minutes, writing down examples in a prominent location.
Now that we've seen a few examples, I'd love for you to take a few minutes to complete your own statements related to your experience and how you will use that experience.	Monitor time and provide clarification as needed.
Would anyone like to share an example?	
Thanks for taking time to reflect with me. Your reflection will help you retain and transfer your experience to your work.	

How to Increase the Value

- Encourage everyone to create If/Then statements for the most difficult concepts or processes in their recent learning experiences.
- Complete this activity in teams. Ask each team to come up with the Ifs and then rotate to another team's If statement to complete the Then statements. Discuss results as a group.

Why I Like This Activity

This appears to be a simple activity, but I've discovered that it holds great value. When we are challenged to see the benefit of taking action, it becomes easier to see why we need to take that action. For example, in a training course for emerging leaders, a participant started her If statement with the phrase, "If I avoid giving feedback when it's uncomfortable." Her peer ended it with, "Then my staff will shut down and lose trust in me." It was an eye-opening moment for her.

A bonus of the activity is that sometimes the statements are surprising and funny. And who doesn't need a bit more lightness in their training days?

If you keep reading, then you'll discover a cringe worthy experience in the next chapter.

Give It a Try

Consider the following phrases and fill in your answers in the space provided. They can relate to your interest in reflection and learning, or to another topic that comes to mind.

If _____, then _____.
If _____, then _____.
If _____, then _____.

NOW ASK YOURSELF

- When could you use If/Then?
- For whom would this activity work well?
- How could you adapt this activity to fit your training program?

Five Whys

If you have been an L&D pro for a while, you have probably used the Five Whys activity. It's an excellent way to help people critically reflect on learning, and it can help participants discover root causes and reveal perspectives they might not have considered on their own.

Five Whys always challenges us to think beyond surface-level observations and see our experiences with a more critical eye. Here's an example:

I want to provide employees with meaningful feedback.
- *Why?* I want team members to see their opportunities for growth and development.
- *Why?* When people see their potential for growth, they are more engaged and satisfied.
- *Why?* When people are engaged and satisfied, they contribute more positively to the organization's culture.
- *Why?* When people contribute more positively to the organization, it creates a better environment for everyone.
- *Why?* When a better environment is created for everyone, we are able to achieve greater results.

AT A GLANCE

Reflection Type
- Individual response, private
- Individual response, publicly shared
- Paired response, publicly shared
- Small group response, publicly shared
- Large group response

Delivery Method
- Virtual instructor-led training
- Instructor-led training
- E-learning
- Self-directed learning

Number of Participants
- Any number

Time Needed
- 15–20 minutes

Reflection Timing
- After

The Activity

You'll ask participants about the portion of the learning experience they've just completed, inviting them to finish the statement "I want to. . . ." regarding something they want to implement. Then, they will respond to the Why? question five times to explore their reasoning and reveal insights about the action.

Step-by-Step Instructions
1. Explain that the Five Whys helps identify the root causes for our actions.
2. Provide an example.
3. Ask everyone to select an insight or a belief they've gained during training. Suggest they review the training objectives or outline.
4. Ask them to ask the question Why? five times, answering each time.
5. Optionally, work together in small groups or as a larger group.

Facilitator's Guide

What to Say	What to Do
Give me a thumbs-up if you've heard of the Five Whys activity.	Acknowledge those who show a thumbs-up.
Choose an insight or a belief from class that you're considering.	
Write down your topic. Use the format, "I want to. . ." or "I need to. . ."	Provide a Five Whys template if you have prepared one.
Ask yourself, "Why?"	
Then, write down your answer.	
Then ask, "Why?" about your answer.	
Now ask, "Why?" again.	
Now ask, "Why?" one final time.	
Take time to consider your responses.	
Ask me if you are stuck or need clarification.	Monitor the room and provide clarification if needed.
Go ahead and wrap up the thought you are on. Thanks for taking time to dig into your whys.	

How to Increase the Value
- Provide groups with the initial topic sentence related to an objective from the learning experience. Ask them to use the Five Whys.
- Conduct a Five Whys rotation. Ask one person to write their topic at the top of a paper or digital document. Rotate the paper to the next person, who responds to the topic before passing it again. The next person responds. When the fifth Why? is answered, return the paper to the original person to review the Five Whys. Discuss as a group.

Why I Like This Activity

- *Why?* Perspective taking is an important element of critical thinking.
- *Why?* It forces us to see from angles we might not otherwise consider.
- *Why?* We are forced to reflect on our thinking, which slows us down.
- *Why?* Thoughtful critical and analytical thinking requires deeper consideration.
- *Why?* We avoid easy, top-of-mind responses as we answer more whys.

Give It a Try

Consider a belief you have about this book or something you've recently learned that you'd like to implement. Answer the first Why? question in the space provided, and then repeat the question four times. When you have finished, take a moment to consider your responses. What do you notice about them? Are you ready to take action?

Your belief or insight: I want to _____

Why? _____

Why? _____

Why? _____

Why? _____

Why? _____

NOW ASK YOURSELF

- When could you use the Five Whys?
- Why would you use it in that instance?
- How could you adapt this activity to fit your training programs?
- Why would you make those adaptations?

Conclusion

Critical thinking grows sharper through effortful reflection. When we explore challenging questions, we develop more rigorous analysis and reasoned conclusions, often questioning our previous actions. In training, encourage the questioning of events and activities, avoiding personal criticism.

Never be afraid of using critical-thinking activities when reflecting, but be prepared to manage the process more carefully. Not everyone will be open to reflecting in this way.

In this chapter, you've reviewed activities to help sharpen critical thinking:

- **Five Questions:** Five journalistic-style questions to frame learning from multiple angles
- **Plan, Monitor, and Evaluate:** A reflection for participants to plan what they want to learn, monitor their progress, and evaluate their outcomes throughout a learning experience
- **What Went Well? What Could Be Better?:** A reflection on experience through answering two simple questions about what went well and what could be improved
- **If/Then:** A reflection that uses If/Then statements to critically consider the consequences of applying new knowledge or skills
- **Five Whys:** A reflection that has participants ask and answer "Why?" five times to explore reasoning and reveal deeper insights about an action or a belief

FINAL QUESTIONS FOR REFLECTION

Think of a learning experience that you anticipate designing or delivering soon, and reflect on how you might use reflection to improve critical thinking.

Ask yourself:

- Which of your learning experiences would benefit from critical-thinking reflection?
- Which activities best fit your programs?
- What modifications do you want to make to any of the activities?

Chapter 10
Outcome 8: Increase Self-Awareness

You are more likely to learn something by finding surprises in your own behavior than by hearing surprising facts about people in general.
—Daniel Kahneman, author, *Thinking, Fast and Slow*

Dear Diary, today THE WORST thing happened.

I wrote that sentence more than once in my childhood diary. In retrospect, I'm certain the "worst thing" was probably not all that bad. I had a relatively uneventful childhood.

Did you keep a childhood diary or journal? Did you mark your childhood tragedies with cringeworthy accounts of life events as a 13-year-old? Were you a list maker or recorder of deep feelings? Did you tuck your journal away in a safe place or did you choose to burn it?

When Dave Nadelberg launched the production *Mortified* at a theater in Portland, Oregon, he tapped into a gold mine of reflection that spread to comedy clubs throughout the United States. *Mortified* is a series of events in which adults read their most embarrassing artifacts from childhood, including "secret diaries, unsent middle-school love letters, song lyrics, art, and even a book report or two" (Edidin 2013).

I believe *Mortified* became so popular because we can all relate. We immediately recognize not just the embarrassment, but also the learning experienced after recording those childhood thoughts and feelings. When we read or listen to outdated, long-abandoned perspectives, we reflect on who we were and who we have become, and that leads to celebrating that we no longer dot our i's with hearts and reinforces our ability to learn and change.

For some of us, youthful experiences writing diaries make us hesitate to continue the practice as adults. If we know we are just going to laugh at our past selves, why bother?

I get it. However, in support of journaling, I would cite a series of studies at Harvard University that found that the value we place on what we record increases over time. A small moment that's easily forgotten does have value to our future selves. The study, *A Present for the Future: The Unexpected Value of Rediscovery*, is worth reading if you want a deeper understanding of reflection as a tool of self-awareness (Zhang et al. 2014)

I've experienced the joy of "rediscovery" by looking through old photos and have watched my family members' delight when they look back at the notes I wrote to go with each photo. Reflection through written and visual artifacts makes us aware of who we were and who we are. Simply put, it gives our past value in the present.

Self-Discovery and Learning That Lasts

The first time I asked people to conduct a coaching conversation with a peer, I was met with resistance. People asked:

- What do we talk about?
- What if they ask me for help?
- How do I respond?

I reassured the group that they would all follow a predetermined question format, and that they'd see how powerful their conversations could be if the coach listened intently and avoided providing advice. Once the awkwardness passed, deep, meaningful conversations occurred. Most people in situations like this discover the value of simply listening, acknowledging, and supporting the person they are coaching.

While we don't always like what we discover about ourselves in the process of reflection, it is essential to our personal and professional development. All reflection requires us to engage in metacognition. Remember, that's the process of thinking about thinking. We use our metacognition abilities to consider our personal biases and tendencies directly. As we think about the way we think, we discover things we might not have realized about ourselves in any other way.

In an ideal world, everyone would reflect on their experiences, identify personal gaps, and discover the motivation to change the behaviors they believe are negative, harmful, or unproductive. Unfortunately, our world is not ideal, and most people don't make time for this kind of self-reflection.

By prompting people to reflect throughout and after a learning experience, we can encourage them to continue this practice and build a habit of reflection. I like the description that Myra Cherchio, CEO of See Vision Eye Institute, shared with me about the power of reflection for self-awareness:

> Reflection is a superpower for leaders with a growth mindset—a strength I've learned to leverage throughout my years as a healthcare executive. I've found that reflection fuels self-awareness, personal growth, and mental resilience. Over time, I've learned that two things can be true: Speed and impact are just as important in business as slowing down to think clearly. In fact, one can fuel the other.

Reflection and taking time to slow down have made me a more effective leader by helping me gain clarity and self-awareness, ultimately increasing my productivity through more thoughtful decision making and intentional action.

A Path to Learning

Remember those dumb things you did when you were a teenager? The lessons didn't resonate in the moment when you were making the mistake, did they? The lessons came later, when you experienced the consequences, sitting alone and thinking back on what you did. In other words, you learned the lesson when you reflected. And maybe, just maybe, you made a different choice the next time.

Now that you've grown out of your teenaged brain, you and the people you interact with can experience greater benefits from reflection. But, it's important to keep in mind that "self-reflection can also become a liability when it morphs into perseverative negative thinking" (Kross et al. 2023). To avoid harmful self-criticism when reflecting on negative experiences, try writing or talking with the universal *you* rather than the more personal *I*.

Activities

Leadership experts James Bailey and Scheherazade Rehman (2022) say, "The practice [of reflection] itself is all about learning, looking back on the day (without bias or regret) to contemplate your behavior and its consequences." Through conversations with 442 executives, they reveal three beneficial areas for self-reflection that we will explore through the activities in this chapter:

- Surprise (cognitive)
- Frustration (emotional)
- Failure (behavioral)

Expect reflection for self-awareness to require more time than previous activities. To maximize people's comfort level, be clear about how they will be asked to share any of their reflections.

> **QUICK QUESTIONS: FACILITATING REFLECTION IN ACTION**
>
> It can be helpful to have quick self-reflection questions ready to ask during training. They might include:
>
> - How do you respond to feedback?
> - What do you value? How do your values align with your organization's?
> - How do you handle mistakes?
> - How do you respond to difficult moments?
> - What situations bring out the best in you? The worst?

Journaling

"Keeping regular work diaries, which took no more than ten minutes a day, gave many of our research participants a new perspective on themselves as professionals and what they needed to improve" (Amabile and Kramer 2011). This was the conclusion of just one of many studies that demonstrate the value of journaling for employees in a wide variety of workplaces.

We remember what we write down. If we can see ourselves transformed by recording an experience, we increase our self-awareness. When our memories fail us, a journal can spark discoveries we might otherwise miss. We can view our shifting thoughts, beliefs, and biases clearly and see improvement over time. Journaling is a powerful tool for several types of learning experiences, including:

- Leadership programs
- Communication programs
- Diversity, equity, inclusion, and accessibility programs

AT A GLANCE

Reflection Type
- Individual response, private

Delivery Method
- Virtual instructor-led training
- Instructor-led training
- E-learning
- Self-directed learning

Number of Participants
- 1 to 1,000

Time Needed
- 5–10 minutes, repeated throughout the program

Reflection Timing
- Before
- During
- After

The Activity

You'll ask participants to choose a place where they will journal—a physical notebook or a digital document they can return to. Throughout your learning experience, pause to encourage everyone to journal their responses to your questions or reflect on what they are feeling or experiencing in the moment. Returning to the same question repeatedly can create a rhythm and familiarity that will help people less comfortable with journaling. Questions to consider include:

- What is resonating with you in the material we have covered?
- How can you implement what you've learned today?
- What are your reservations about what we've covered?

Also consider encouraging free-form journaling, in which participants just write whatever comes to mind. This works well for people who are already accustomed to journaling but may be more difficult for those new to it.

Step-by-Step Instructions

1. Ask everyone to find a place to journal. Encourage the use of a physical notebook or digital document that they can easily return to throughout the learning experience.
2. Explain the benefit of journaling as a reflective practice.
3. Provide prompts or ask participants to do free-form journaling.
4. Let everyone know they will not be required to share what they write.
5. Ask participants to take three to five minutes to write their thoughts.
6. Invite them to write in their journal throughout the learning experience and when they return to the job.

Facilitator's Guide

What to Say	What to Do
Please choose a place you can write your thoughts. A notebook or document you can easily return is ideal.	
Here is a prompt. [*Or, here are a series of prompts or we are going to do some free-form journaling about any topic you choose.*]	Provide one or several journaling prompts or allow participants to choose their topic.
Take the next five minutes to write your thoughts. They are private and won't be shared with anyone. I won't ask you to give them to me. They are yours.	Set a 5-minute timer. Monitor the group, answering any questions.
Please wrap up the thought you are on. I'll periodically ask you to return to your journal as we work through our time together.	

How to Increase the Value

- Provide journaling prompts relevant to each portion of your training program. Consider selecting one prompt per objective.
- Add a short debrief for the whole group after the journaling period. Ask for any reactions people want to share.
- Consider using the Five Questions activity from chapter 9 as a basis for journaling.

Why I Like This Activity

I heard a collective groan when I told the 24 people in an emerging-leader program to journal each week of our 10-week program. Because journaling is an important leadership practice, one of the program's goals was to help potential new managers create a journaling habit.

While the activity was initially met with frustration, the participants who stuck to it throughout our time together saw an undeniable benefit when they reviewed moments of personal insight that they might have otherwise missed.

I didn't ask them to share their journals with one another, but I did invite them to talk about the process. I'd happily listen to the groan again to gain the benefits of journaling.

Give It a Try

Set a timer for five minutes and write your reflections about one of these topics in the space provided:
- What is the value of what you've read in this book so far?
- How can you incorporate more reflection into your workflows each day?
- How will people in the training programs you conduct or on your L&D team react to being asked to reflect more intentionally?
- How have you benefited from reflection?

NOW ASK YOURSELF

- What do you like about Journaling for reflection?
- When could you use Journaling for reflection?
- Which learning experiences would journaling work well for?

The Coaching Conversation

Have you ever been asked a single question that made you see your situation in a new way? If you answered yes, you've experienced the power of coaching. The best coaching doesn't provide answers but instead provides thoughtful questions that help us better understand our beliefs, values, and options. Coaching can change us.

As L&D pros, we can bring informal coaching to a learning experience through a series of reflective questions to help people discover how they can implement new knowledge and skills. Good coaching requires constantly practicing communication skills and developing our emotional intelligence, something we all can benefit from.

In this activity, I've been inspired by Michael Bungay Stanier's question-coaching format. I recommend taking a look at his books *The Coaching Habit* and *The Advice Trap*.

AT A GLANCE

Reflection Type
- Paired response, private
- Paired response, publicly shared

Delivery Method
- Virtual instructor-led training
- Instructor-led training

Number of Participants
- Any number

Time Needed
- 10–20 minutes

Reflection Timing
- During
- After

The Activity

You will put participants in pairs, with one person acting as the coach and the other as the coaching client. Provide a list of questions to prompt discussion. Halfway through the activity, the coach and client will switch roles. Encourage everyone to follow these rules:

- The designated coach asks the questions one at a time.
- Focus more on listening than holding a conversation.
- Add additional questions prompted by listening to the client's answers.

The process will feel awkward at first, but during the coaching conversation, participants will discover new things about themselves. Encourage them to share their experiences in the debrief after the activity.

Step-by-Step Instructions

1. Put participants into pairs.
2. Explain the coaching questions, their benefits, and how reflection helps self-awareness.
3. Ask one person in each group to act as the coach, asking questions and considering the answers. Let them know they will switch roles halfway through the activity so everyone can be coached.
4. Provide questions.
5. Monitor time and tell participants to switch roles at the halfway mark. Provide clarification as needed.
6. Debrief after the coaching activity with questions, including:
   - What stood out for you as you were coached?
   - How did you feel about being coached?
   - What value did coaching have for you?
   - What will you do differently when you return to work?

Facilitator's Guide

What to Say	What to Do
We are going to take about 10 minutes for a coaching conversation. This is a form of reflection to help increase self-awareness and practice a coaching technique.	Pair everyone up, using breakout rooms if the session is virtual.
I'll provide you with questions. When you are the coach, please use these questions and actively listen to your partner's responses.	Set a timer and monitor the time
It's OK to ask additional questions.	
[At the halfway point] Please switch roles so everyone can be coached.	
Let me know if you have questions or need clarification.	The second coach begins asking questions. Continue monitoring time.
Wrap up your conversations. Let's come back together now.	
Let's take a moment and discuss your experience. • What stood out when you were coached? • How did you feel about being coached? • What value did coaching have for you? • What will you do differently when you return to work?	Lead the debrief.
Thanks for your time and effort coaching.	

How to Increase the Value

- Consider beginning and ending your programs with coaching conversations, keeping the same pairs throughout the program. These relationships foster deeper connection while also providing opportunities for self-awareness.

Why I Like This Activity

My friend Paul Briley hosts the *Off the Comma* podcast, which gives people (including me) a chance to share their stories of feeling stuck and trying to get unstuck. These conversations invariably become moments of reflection when Paul, a seasoned and talented coach, moves his guests through thoughtful and sometimes difficult discussions of events in their lives.

My time with Paul led to tears, and I "discovered the comma I was sitting on." I ultimately found the courage to move forward because of our coaching conversation. Paul's careful use of questions tailor-made for the situation was a great lesson in self-awareness. My experience with Paul became my catalyst for contacting a publisher and writing the book you are reading.

Give It a Try

Try a coaching conversation with yourself by answering the questions in the space provided.

- What's on your mind?

- And what else?

- What is the real challenge here for you?

- What do you want?

- If you are saying yes to this opportunity, what are you saying no to?

NOW ASK YOURSELF

- When could you use the Coaching Conversation?
- Who could benefit from the Coaching Conversation?
- How could you adapt this activity to fit your training programs?

Your Best Experience

What was your best experience in the workplace? Does a moment come to mind immediately, or do you need more time to think about it? We tend to focus on the worst of our experiences, but what if we switched our focus to the best of our experiences?

Your Best Experience is based on the Appreciative Inquiry method, developed by David Cooperrider at Case Western Reserve University. By asking questions about our best times, we can learn to create more of them. Appreciative Inquiry has been used in a variety of situations from kindergarten classes to the US Navy. The process starts with interviews in which we share stories about our best experiences, our values, and the wishes we have for the future. It's a positive reflective process that moves us to action.

You may remember that, early in the book, I suggested avoiding asking for "bests" and "worsts," but for this particular activity, asking for "bests" works well.

AT A GLANCE

Reflection Type
- Paired response, publicly shared
- Small group response, publicly shared

Delivery Method
- Virtual instructor-led training
- Instructor-led training

Number of Participants
- 1 to 25

Time Needed
- 10–15 minutes
- Reduce the number of questions to reduce the time this reflection takes

Reflection Timing
- Before
- During
- After

The Activity

In this activity, you'll provide pairs with questions that allow them to explore their best experiences related to your training topic. The discussion happens in an interview style, with one person asking a question and documenting the answers. Then, the roles are switched so each person has a chance to act as the questioner. In a final group discussion, everyone shares the highlights of their paired conversations. From the highlights, specific actions are identified that everyone can take moving forward. By identifying the best results, people take carefully considered steps to do more of what has worked.

Step-by-Step Instructions

1. Form small groups of two to three people. Pairs are ideal.
2. Describe the concept of Appreciative Inquiry.
3. Explain that members of each group will interview one another using Appreciative Inquiry questions, with each person getting a chance to take on the role of questioner.
4. Encourage them to keep notes of conversation highlights and "quotable quotes."
5. After the interviews, invite groups to share a few highlights.
6. Lead the group through a discussion about what actions they can take to make more "best experiences" happen when they return to work.
7. Record actions in a visible location.

Facilitator's Guide

What to Say	What to Do
How often do you take time to appreciate the best things around you?	
We are now going to take about 15 minutes to do just that. We're going to explore the best of our experiences related to [*insert your topic*].	Customize for your topic.
Appreciative Inquiry is the process of looking at our best experiences so we can create more of them. It's a process used by groups ranging from the US Navy to kindergarten classes.	
We are going to form groups of two or three people. In your groups, I'd like you to interview one another with a set of questions I'll provide. Keep notes of the highlights and quotable quotes. Remember, it's an interview, not a discussion. Ask probing questions but avoid sharing your story or perspective if it's not your turn.	Form groups of two or three people. Provide the interview questions either in handout form or as a visual on a screen.
Join your partner [*or partners*], introduce yourself, and begin your interviews.	Monitor groups and provide clarification as needed.

What to Say	What to Do
We've reached the turning point. Please switch interviewers if you haven't yet.	Monitor groups and provide clarification as needed. Repeat this switch if you have groups of three people.
Wrap up your conversations. Let's come back together.	
I'd love to hear the highlights of your conversations.	Record highlights of conversations in a visible location.
What actions do these highlights show us you can take when you return to work in order to experience more "bests"?	Record actions in a visible location.
Thanks for taking the time to explore your best experiences.	

How to Increase the Value
- Invite interview groups to find a comfortable location to interview one another, encouraging walking interviews if manageable for the group's location.
- After interviews, combine two interview groups to share highlights and stories. Ask them to find common themes in all their stories to share with the larger group.
- Visit the Appreciative Inquiry Commons for more questions and information about Appreciative Inquiry, at appreciativeinquiry.champlain.edu.

Why I Like This Activity
Something magical occurs when an entire roomful of people are sharing their best experiences. The noise level increases, and the joy is palpable. This activity is always a pleasure to facilitate. While everyone is reflecting on their best experience, a clear list of practical actions for the future often materializes.

The values question can be difficult for many people—values are often unconscious—but the reflection they experience can lead to better self-awareness. Because this activity is an interview rather than a discussion, many people find the level of listening and engagement refreshing and unusual.

Give It a Try

Consider the following questions and answer them in the space provided.

Your Best Experience

- What is the best experience you've had as a result of reflecting on your own learning?

- What do you value about reflection?

- If you could be granted three wishes related to your reflection practice in the future, what would they be?
    - »
    - »
    - »

NOW ASK YOURSELF

- When could you use Your Best Experience?

- Which groups would this work well for?

- How could you adapt this activity to fit your training programs?

What I Thought, What I Think

Have you ever written a letter to your future self? I've been part of many programs that require this sort of letter to help clarify future actions and current thinking. What I Thought, What I Think is based on this idea, but with a twist.

At the beginning of a learning experience, participants will assess their current thinking. At the end of the program (or a future date when they've had time to transfer and implement what they've learned), they'll assess their thinking again. This should reveal the changes in their thinking before and after the learning experience.

AT A GLANCE

Reflection Type
- Individual response, private
- Individual response, publicly shared
- Paired response, private
- Paired response, publicly shared
- Small group response, private
- Small group response, publicly shared

Delivery Method
- Virtual instructor-led training
- Instructor-led training
- E-learning
- Self-directed learning

Number of Participants
- Any number

Time Needed
- 3–5 minutes for individual reflection
- 10–15 minutes for group reflection

Reflection Timing
- Before
- After

The Activity

You will ask everyone to assess their initial understanding of and feelings about a concept or work process before or at an early stage in the learning experience. At the end of the program, everyone will reassess their knowledge and feelings using the same set of questions. They will then compare their before-and-after assessments.

You can expand the activity with small group discussions to debrief with additional reflection questions that reveal how the group's knowledge and thinking have changed.

Step-by-Step Instructions

1. Provide everyone with a brief assessment related to the topic.
2. Give them time to assess their understanding and feelings.
3. At the conclusion of training, provide the same assessment.

4. Once the second assessment is completed, ask everyone to compare their two assessments.
5. Discuss what they noticed, how they changed, and what the change means for them.

Facilitator's Guide

What to Say	What to Do
I am going to give you a quick assessment to see what you know and how you feel about our topic today.	Provide a digital or analog assessment for everyone. As an alternative, you may provide the assessment before your first meeting.
This information is for your eyes only. At the end of our time together, you'll take the assessment again to see what changes have occurred.	
Give me a thumbs-up when you are done.	Monitor the group for completion and to answer any questions.
Now put the assessment aside somewhere you can easily find it again and return to at the end of training.	
[*At the conclusion of training*] Let's take a quick assessment like the one you did at the beginning of the program. After you complete this, we'll compare it to your first assessment.	Provide the final assessment. Monitor completion and clarify any questions.
Now that you've finished the assessment, let's compare your before and after.	
What did you notice when you compared the two assessments?	Lead a discussion exploring the changes from the beginning to the end of the program.
What's the value in comparing the before and after?	Continue the discussion, jotting down key points in a visible location.
Thanks for taking the time to reflect on your experience.	

How to Increase the Value

- After training, remind everyone to review their assessments in two or three months to see how they've changed after returning to work.
- Compile the group's responses and share an aggregate view of the before and after. Make sure to request permission to use everyone's responses in this way.

Why I Like This Activity

Self-awareness begins with a careful examination of our own thinking. This activity leads participants methodically through that process.

I've seen the value of people returning to something they wrote to see how they've changed through a learning experience. It often reveals biases they carried. At the end of an emerging-leader course, one participant shared that she wasn't ready to be a leader. Comparing what she thought leading others took with what she had learned showed her areas she wanted to develop before taking on leadership responsibilities.

I love watching people when they become more self-aware.

Give It a Try

It's time to assess your current thinking. In the provided example, select the number that best describes you and fill in the blanks with words that come to mind.

What I Thought, What I Think

Initial Reflection

1. My use of reflection for learning (circle your response)

   0　　　1　　　2　　　3　　　4　　　5
   Never　　　　　　　　　　　　　　Frequent

2. My knowledge of the science of reflection (circle your response)

   0　　　1　　　2　　　3　　　4　　　5
   Never　　　　　　　　　　　　　　Frequent

3. Reflection is _____

4. When should reflection occur? (circle your response)

   Before　　　　During　　　　After
   learning　　　learning　　　learning

Complete the following section after you've finished reading.

Final Reflection

1. My use of reflection for learning (circle your response)

   0　　　1　　　2　　　3　　　4　　　5
   Never　　　　　　　　　　　　　　Frequent

2. My knowledge of the science of reflection (circle your response)

   0　　　1　　　2　　　3　　　4　　　5
   Never　　　　　　　　　　　　　　Frequent

Compare Reflections

1. What changes do you notice between your initial and final reflections?
2. What changes occurred between your initial and final reflections?

NOW ASK YOURSELF

- When could you use What I Thought, What I Think?
- Which groups would this work well for?
- How could you adapt this activity to fit your training programs?

Surprise, Failure, and Frustration

What we focus on when we reflect matters. This activity is based on the three key themes that researchers James Bailey and Scheherazade Rehman (2022) identified in their research with executives. By focusing on what surprises us and the failures and frustrations we've experienced, we can create new opportunities for self-improvement.

AT A GLANCE

Reflection Type
- Individual response, private
- Individual response, publicly shared
- Small group response, private
- Small group response, publicly shared

Delivery Method
- Virtual instructor-led training
- Instructor-led training
- E-learning
- Self-directed learning

Number of Participants
- Any number

Time Needed
- 6–10 minutes for personal reflection
- 10 minutes for small group discussion

Reflection Timing
- During
- After

The Activity

You will encourage everyone to consider questions about distinct experiences they've had that have sparked feelings of surprise, failure, and frustration. They will first reflect individually and then share in pairs or small groups. Encourage another review of the questions when the participants return to work. These three questions can also be used as journaling prompts.

Step-by-Step Instructions

1. Let all participants know they are going to take time to reflect on their experiences by considering three key questions.
2. Explain the relevance of the three questions, citing the research if appropriate for your participants.
3. Ask everyone to take time to write their responses. Explain they will not be required to share, but modify this if you plan on splitting them into small groups.
4. When everyone appears done or time is up, ask quick debrief questions:
   - What dd you notice as you answered the questions?
   - What was the value of writing your responses?

Facilitator's Guide

What to Say	What to Do
We are going to take 10 minutes to reflect on your experiences with three key questions to consider.	
Find a place you can record your responses. Make sure it's somewhere you can easily find in the future.	Provide everyone with writing material or suggest digital writing tools.
The three questions you see are the questions the most successful executives revealed as crucial to their individual development and success.	Show the questions.
Please consider and answer the questions. You won't be required to share your responses with anyone.	Monitor time and provide any clarification needed.
[*Alternatively*]: After you've considered your questions, you'll form small groups so you can share your responses. You can, of course, pass on sharing anything you aren't comfortable sharing.	
Thanks for taking time to consider the questions. Let's take a few minutes to talk about your experience. • What did you notice as you answered the questions? • What was the value of writing your responses?	Lead a debrief discussion, waiting for responses from the group.

How to Increase the Value

- At the end of the activity, form small groups of three to four people and ask them to discuss their responses to the questions. Make sure they know they do not have to share any responses they are not comfortable sharing.
- Encourage journaling as an additional activity when everyone returns to work.
- Plan future follow-ups with everyone to review their questions.

THE RESEARCH

To identify the most valuable forms of reflection, Bailey and Rehman surveyed 442 executives about the experiences that most influenced their leadership success. The responses were coded (and reviewed twice) to find sentimental themes. Reflections that contained surprises, failures, and frustrations showed the most value to the leader's professional development.

Why I Like This Activity

This activity is based on research showing that reflection supports self-development. I love that strong link to the science, as well as the vulnerability this activity requires.

While it is easy for me to find an example of surprise and frustration, I often struggle with failure, and so do many people. The struggle is not because I haven't failed, but because admitting failure is difficult, even when it presents a learning opportunity. So, it's important to give people extra time and a little grace in answering these questions.

Give It a Try

Consider and answer the following questions in the space provided. You can use reading this book, your personal practice of reflection, or an issue you are grappling with currently.

Surprise, Failure, and Frustration

Surprise
Think of a recent situation that surprised you. How did it challenge your expectations or assumptions? What did you learn from your experience?

Failure
Recall a recent failure or setback. What went wrong? Why? How did you respond? What would you do differently next time?

Frustration
Think of a situation that caused you frustration recently. What was the source of the frustration? How did you manage your emotions? What could you do to handle similar situations in the future?

NOW ASK YOURSELF

- When could you use Surprise, Failure, and Frustration?
- Which groups would this work well for?
- How could you adapt this activity to fit your training programs?

Conclusion

Self-awareness is the cornerstone of success in all our organizations. If you know yourself, you will be more successful working with others.

Working with self-aware colleagues increases our empathy and enhances psychological safety in the workplace. Encouraging reflection that guides people to explore who they are and how they act in the workplace benefits everyone. As L&D professionals, we often see the inclusion of self-reflection in leadership, diversity, and personal development training as logical, but we may want to consider including it as part of other programs.

In this chapter, we explored five self-reflection activities:

- **Journaling:** Writing down thoughts, experiences, and insights
- **The Coaching Conversation:** A paired activity in which participants take turns asking powerful questions
- **Your Best Experience:** An Appreciative Inquiry–based activity in which participants interview one another about their best experiences related to a specific topic, focusing on future action
- **What I Thought, What I Think:** A before-and-after assessment activity to compare initial thoughts and feelings about a topic with perspectives after a learning experience
- **Surprise, Failure, and Frustration:** Considering experiences of surprise, failure, and frustration to gain deeper self-insight and identify areas for improvement

Like many of the activities included in other chapters, these activities will benefit participants beyond the training room. When we can encourage building an ongoing reflection habit, people will experience more lasting and meaningful learning outcomes.

FINAL QUESTIONS FOR REFLECTION

Think of a learning experience you anticipate designing or delivering soon and reflect on how you might use reflection to improve self-awareness.

Ask yourself:

- Which activities work best for your programs?
- What unique qualities do participants have that you need to consider when selecting activities?
- What modifications do you want to make to any of the activities?

Conclusion

> When you take time to reflect and plan . . . you're saying
> something is important: My choices matter.
> My direction matters. What I want matters.
> —Chris Guillebeau, author, *Time Anxiety* and *The Happiness of Pursuit*

You made it to the final pages. Getting here took both of us a lot of time and effort. As I wrote each chapter nearing the conclusion, I questioned my perspectives about reflection as well as my views on learning and development. Was it better to call people *learners, participants,* or something else? Should I refer to a *learning experience, training, facilitation,* or something else? I sometimes teetered on the line between reflection and rumination. However, I never questioned my firm belief that reflection helps create learning that lasts.

What did you question as you made your way through the pages? How has your perspective on reflection changed? What new ways of using reflection in your work have you discovered?

At this point, you know how reflection can affect performance, boost motivation, and increase self-awareness, among other benefits. Whether you choose to include reflection during the beginning, middle, or close of a learning experience, you've seen the importance of writing well-crafted prompts and the power of pausing for people to think more deeply and critically. You can ask participants to journal, fold paper in interesting configurations, or list what they already know about a topic. Reflection changes how we learn, which in turn can change behaviors in the workplace.

With advances in technology, it's easy to overlook the simple tools that help learning last. Reflection is one of the oldest, most useful tools available to us, with the bonus of costing nothing more than time and thoughtful effort. I hope you agree that reflection is a tool that's fundamental for learning and development.

Karl Kapp (2022) has pointed out that reflection is also one of the skills needed for the development of wisdom: "Being wise means you are able to slow down, simultaneously reflecting on the moment, looking beyond the moment, and distilling the moment."

After you've read these pages and perhaps embarked on your own ongoing reflection practice, I believe you have more wisdom than you started with. You can now share that wisdom with your peers and the participants for whom you are designing and delivering learning experiences.

Whether a learning experience requires a 30-minute virtual session or an ongoing blended learning approach, reflection will help create a lasting impact on participants and, ultimately, their organizations.

Before you close this book, take a moment to reflect on a few final questions:
- What words and phrases can you easily recall from these pages?
- How are you feeling as you wrap up this book?
- What have you learned from reading this book?
- What new practices do you plan to put in place after reading this book?
- How would you describe this book to a friend (or a five-year-old)?
- And finally, what is your definition of *reflection*?

Thanks for pausing to go on this reflection adventure with me. I hope it benefits you now and well into the future. Please reach out to me with your reflections about what you've read and anything you might be wondering about reflection. I look forward to hearing from you.

For now, reflect on, my friend! You are amazing.

Before you put this book down,
pause for a moment.

What did you gain
from the pages of this book?

Acknowledgments

When I've read book acknowledgments in the past, I've always wondered, "How do people know so many people?" I imagined I'd thank my mom and dad, my spouse, and my child. I'd mention a few friends and, of course, my editor. And that would be the end of my list.

Then I wrote a book. With every step of the process, I've connected with one more person who willingly and eagerly extended their support. Their generosity and kindness has renewed my faith in humanity. I've seen evidence that the world is filled with caring people who promote and amplify the work of others.

So, let me reflect on the community of people who've made this book possible.

Paul Briley, you asked me the questions that moved me "off the comma." The day after our conversation, I made the call that led to these pages. You are good at what you do, my friend.

Alexandria Clapp, thank you for answering my emotional call and getting Jack Harlow on the line. You've continued to champion ME. I'm grateful for you and the energy you bring to all your work.

Jack, thank you for being one of the kindest humans I know. You didn't laugh when I sent you a 200-page document that was disconnected and unfocused. Your sincerity as we worked through ideas before landing on reflection is appreciated.

Jack and I found the reflection topic after reading Karl Kapp's clever post about wisdom. Thank you, Karl, for sharing your wisdom and inspiring this book.

Once I began to form my book ideas, I stalked every author's signing at Learning Guild and ATD events. Thank you to JD Dillon, Robyn Defelice, Sarah Mercier, and Kimberli Jeter for answering my questions and sharing your perspective. (I'd also like to point out that both JD and Karl are named in my book. IYKYK.)

Thank you to Cindy Huggett and Kassie LaBorie for treating me like a colleague while I fan-girled during our first meeting. Cindy, you offered support throughout the writing process, and knowing you are in my corner means the world to me. Kassie, you helped me find my eight buckets and shared advice on how to fill them. You are just as inspiring as Mel Robbins.

Thank you, MJ Hall. Our discussion and the ATD Forum resources you shared were essential in getting my ideas in order and deepening my understanding of reflection.

Sue Landay, how have you not been my friend for decades? I appreciate our chats, your Trainers Warehouse resources, and your support. I hope we can continue to swap stories of our children and L&D.

I'm grateful for every person who has participated in every training program I've offered for the last 28 years. You've taught me so much about L&D and myself. You've shared your stories, laughed at my jokes, and endured the success and failures of my experimental activities.

Thank you, Michelle Petro, for being an outstanding producer and friend. You've tolerated my experiments and last-minute schedule adjustments.

There are so many people to thank who often believed in my ideas more than I did. Brittany Tezanos-Pinto—you listened to all the stories of my book writing journey. Your company and coffee got me through it!

Rosalind Sago, you've believed in me longer than I've believed in myself. Thank you for your support and encouragement.

Katie Valdivia, 20 years ago you didn't know me, but you didn't hesitate to solve the problem I created when I showed up at the wrong location. You are a class act and dear friend. Our conversations and your willingness to try innovative things have shaped who I am as a facilitator and consultant.

Thank you, Holly Burkett, the person I only see when I fly 2,000 miles away from home even though we live within 20 minutes of each other. I'm so lucky you introduced me to Elaine Beich. Elaine, this book took me more than two weeks to write, but you inspired me throughout. Next book, I'm taking your advice.

I'm indebted to the Let's Learn Together Community and the L&D Book Group for providing a space where we can experiment, explore, commiserate, and laugh. I wish I could name all of you, but we'd run out of paper. Thank you specifically to Jessica Branum, Susanne Brabeck, and Lisa Bacon for being the voices of reason and staying for the after party. And to Neil Ifill for always making me laugh.

Thank you to the Sacramento ATD Chapter for being my home and my cheering squad. I appreciate you. Juliette and Jen—you are amazing!

Erin Lebacqz, thank you for being my friend and for connecting me to Anne Janzer. Anne, thank you for sharing your wise words with the world and for your support. Your books were my companions through my writing journey.

To my Conspiracy chapter group—Mohamed Osman, Daniel Moore, and Daniele O'Leary. Sharing our worthy goals was powerful practice in vulnerability and accountability. Thank you for listening. We are enough.

Thank you, Jess Almlie and Robyn Defelice. You were the support I needed through this process. I'm grateful to you both for giving so openly and responding to my long texts.

Thanks to the team at ATD Press for all you do. What an adventure it's been.

Without the corner table at Milka Coffee Roasters, I'd still be working on this manuscript. Thank you to the staff for knowing my name and my order. Many days I spent more time with you than with my family.

To my third-grade teacher, Mrs. King. I wrote a book! You believed in me then and that propelled me to today. Thank you.

And to my family—biological and chosen.

How do I thank someone who helped me create the original outline, took time to edit chapters, who checked on my progress, and only laughed a little when I chopped my favorite rose bush to the ground in frustration over the editing process? Thank you, Meghan. I'm lucky you were on social media long enough to become my friend.

Mom, thanks for leaving me at the library (and eventually remembering to pick me up). The library opened a world of words and possibility. And Dad, thanks for making stories a part of who I am.

Thank you, Connor. You've played my reflection games your entire life. I forgive you for the year you were 13 and love you more than ever in your 20th year. Your perseverance, self-advocacy, and amazing mind teach me so much. I am excited for the opportunity to reflect together as you create your path in this world.

And finally, to Shea. You've always been the one. You read every chapter of this book (some more than once) and have propped me up more times than I can count. There is nothing for me but to love you.

Appendix A
Activities at a Glance

This appendix presents key information about the activities in each outcome to help you select the ones that best meet your needs.

For each activity, you'll find:
- The suggested number of participants
- The general amount of time needed
- When to perform the activity
- The suggested instructional format
- The reflection type

Activity	Number of Participants	Time Needed	Reflection Timing	Instructional Format	Reflection Type
Outcome 1. Boost Motivation to Learn					
Prior Knowledge Mental Inventory	• Unlimited	• Short • Medium	• Before	• Virtual instructor-led training • Instructor-led training • E-learning • Self-directed learning	• Individual response, publicly shared • Small group response, publicly shared • Large group response
Quiz Me!	• Unlimited	• Medium	• Before	• Virtual instructor-led training • Instructor-led training • E-learning • Self-directed learning	• Individual response, private • Individual response, shared anonymously
Finish the Sentence	• Unlimited	• Medium	• Before • During • After	• Virtual instructor-led training • Instructor-led training • E-learning • Self-directed learning	• Individual response, private • Individual response, publicly shared • group response, publicly shared
I'm Curious About . . .	• Unlimited	• Short • Medium	• Before	• Virtual instructor-led training • Instructor-led training • E-learning • Self-directed learning	• Individual response, private • Individual response, publicly shared • Small response, publicly shared
Outcome 2. Build Social Connection					
Individual Learning Maps	• Unlimited	• Medium	• During • After	• Virtual instructor-led training • Instructor-led training • E-learning • Self-directed learning	• Individual response, private • Individual response, publicly shared
Small Group Learning Maps	• Small	• Long	• During • After	• Virtual instructor-led training • Instructor-led training	• Small group response, publicly shared

Activity	Number of Participants	Time Needed	Reflection Timing	Instructional Format	Reflection Type
Shared Learning Map	• Small • Unlimited	• Long	• During • After	• Virtual instructor-led training • Instructor-led training • E-learning	• Large group response
I Would Title This . . .	• Unlimited	• Medium	• Before	• Virtual instructor-led training • Instructor-led training	• Individual response, publicly shared • Small group response, publicly shared
Draw a Mind Map	• Unlimited	• Medium	• During • After	• Virtual instructor-led training • Instructor-led training • E-learning • Self-directed learning	• Individual response, private • Individual response, publicly shared • Small group response, publicly shared • Large response
Reflect, Pair, Share	• Unlimited	• Long	• During • After	• Virtual instructor-led training • Instructor-led training	• Individual response, publicly shared • Paired response, private • Paired response, publicly shared • Small group response, private • Small group response, publicly shared
Outcome 3. Strengthen Memory					
Five Bullet Points	• Unlimited	• Medium	• During • After	• Virtual instructor-led training • Instructor-led training • E-learning • Self-directed learning	• Individual response, private • Individual response, publicly shared • Small group response, publicly shared
One Question	• Small groups	• Short • Long	• During • After	• Virtual instructor-led training • Instructor-led training	• Individual response, publicly shared

Appendix A

Activity	Number of Participants	Time Needed	Reflection Timing	Instructional Format	Reflection Type
The Spinning Wheel of Wonder	• Small • Medium • Large	• Medium	• During • After	• Virtual instructor-led training • Instructor-led training	• Large group response
Fill In Your Box	• Small • Medium • Large	• Medium	• During • After	• Virtual instructor-led training	• Individual response, publicly shared
Draw Your Thought	• Unlimited	• Medium	• During • After	• Virtual instructor-led training • Instructor-led training • E-learning • Self-directed learning	• Individual response, private
What's it Like	• Unlimited	• Short • Medium	• During • After	• Virtual instructor-led training • Instructor-led training	• Individual response, private • Individual response, publicly shared • Paired response, publicly shared • Small group response, publicly shared
Outcome 4. Create Deeper Insight					
Take Two Minutes	• Unlimited	• Short	• During • After	• Virtual instructor-led training • Instructor-led training • E-learning • Self-directed learning	• Individual response, private • Individual response, shared anonymously • Individual response, publicly shared
R&R	• Unlimited	• Medium	• During • After	• Virtual instructor-led training • Instructor-led training • E-learning • Self-directed learning	• Individual response, private • Individual response, publicly shared • Paired response, private • Paired response, publicly shared • Small group response, private • Small group response, publicly shared

Activity	Number of Participants	Time Needed	Reflection Timing	Instructional Format	Reflection Type
Instructional Origami	• Unlimited	• Long	• Before • During • After	• Virtual instructor-led training • Instructor-led training • E-learning • Self-directed learning	• Individual response, private
Four Corners	• Unlimited	• Medium	• After	• Virtual instructor-led training • Instructor-led training • E-learning • Self-directed learning	• Individual response, private • Individual response, publicly shared • Small group response, publicly shared • Large group response
Before and After	• Unlimited	• Medium	• Before • During • After	• Virtual instructor-led training • Instructor-led training	• Individual response, private • Individual response, publicly shared
What? Gut? So What? Now What?	• Unlimited	• Medium	• During • After	• Virtual instructor-led training • Instructor-led training • E-learning • Self-directed learning	• Individual response, publicly shared • Large group response
Wonder Wall	• Small • Medium	• Medium	• Before • During • After	• Virtual instructor-led training • Instructor-led training	• Individual response, shared anonymously • Individual response, publicly shared
Tell Me a Story	• Small • Medium • Unlimited	• Medium	• During • After	• Virtual instructor-led training • Instructor-led training	• Paired response, private • Paired response, publicly shared • Small group response, private • Small group response, publicly shared

Activity	Number of Participants	Time Needed	Reflection Timing	Instructional Format	Reflection Type
Explain It to a Five-Year-Old	• Small • Medium • Unlimited	• Medium	• During • After	• Virtual instructor-led training • Instructor-led training	• Paired response, private • Paired response, publicly shared • Small group response, private • Small group response, publicly shared
Outcome 5. Assess Progress					
The Chat Cascade	• Small • Medium • Unlimited	• Short	• During • After	• Virtual instructor-led training	• Individual response, publicly shared
On a Scale of 1 to 5	• Unlimited	• Short	• During • After	• Virtual instructor-led training • Instructor-led training	• Individual response, shared anonymously • Individual response, publicly shared
I Like, I Wish, I Wonder	• Unlimited	• Medium	• During • After	• Virtual instructor-led training • Instructor-led training	• Individual response, private • Paired response, private • Small group response, private
Just One Word	• Unlimited	• Short	• During • After	• Virtual instructor-led training • Instructor-led training	• Individual response, publicly shared
I'll Use/Tell Me More	• Unlimited	• Medium	• During • After	• Virtual instructor-led training • Instructor-led training	• Individual response, shared anonymously
Outcome 6. Improve Performance					
Insight and Action	• Unlimited	• Medium	• After	• Virtual instructor-led training • Instructor-led training	• Individual response, private • Individual response, publicly shared • Small group response, private • Small group response, publicly shared • Large group response

Activity	Number of Participants	Time Needed	Reflection Timing	Instructional Format	Reflection Type
Start, Stop, Continue	• Unlimited	• Medium • Long	• After	• Virtual instructor-led training • Instructor-led training	• Individual response, private • Individual response, publicly shared • Paired response, private • Paired response, publicly shared • Small group response, private • Small group response, publicly shared • Large group response
It's a RAP	• Unlimited	• Long	• After	• Virtual instructor-led training • Instructor-led training • E-learning • Self-directed learning	• Individual response, private
Pause, Breathe, Think	• Unlimited	• Short	• Before • During • After	• Virtual instructor-led training • Instructor-led training • E-learning • Self-directed learning	• Individual response, private • Individual response, publicly shared • Large group response
Just Imagine	• Unlimited	• Short • Medium	• During • After	• Virtual instructor-led training • Instructor-led training • E-learning • Self-directed learning	• Individual response, private • Individual response, publicly shared
After-Action Review	• Small • Medium • Large	• Long	• After	• Virtual instructor-led training • Instructor-led training	• Individual response, private • Large group response

Appendix A

Activity	Number of Participants	Time Needed	Reflection Timing	Instructional Format	Reflection Type
Outcome 7. Sharpen Critical Thinking					
Five Questions	• Unlimited	• Long	• After	• Virtual instructor-led training • Instructor-led training • E-learning • Self-directed learning	• Individual response, private • Individual response, publicly shared • Paired response, private • Paired response, publicly shared • Small group response, private • Small group response, publicly shared • Larger group response
Plan, Monitor, and Evaluate	• Unlimited	• Short	• Before • During • After	• Virtual instructor-led training • Instructor-led training • E-learning • Self-directed learning	• Individual response, private • Individual response, publicly shared
What Went Well? What Could Be Better?	• Unlimited	• Medium	• After	• Virtual instructor-led training • Instructor-led training • E-learning • Self-directed learning	• Individual response, private • Paired response, private • Small group response, private • Larger group response
If/Then	• Unlimited	• Short • Long	• Before • During • After	• Virtual instructor-led training • Instructor-led training • E-learning • Self-directed learning	• Individual response, private • Paired response, private • Small group response, private • Larger group response
Five Whys	• Unlimited	• Long	• After	• Virtual instructor-led training • Instructor-led training • E-learning • Self-directed learning	• Individual response, private • Individual response, publicly shared • Paired response, publicly shared • Small group response, publicly shared • Large group response

Activity	Number of Participants	Time Needed	Reflection Timing	Instructional Format	Reflection Type
Outcome 8. Increase Self-Awareness					
Journaling	• Small • Medium • Large	• Medium	• Before • During • After	• Virtual instructor-led training • Instructor-led training • E-learning • Self-directed learning	• Individual response, private
The Coaching Conversation	• Unlimited	• Long	• During • After	• Virtual instructor-led training • Instructor-led training	• Paired response, private • Paired response, publicly shared
Your Best Experience	• Unlimited	• Long	• Before • During • After	• Virtual instructor-led training • Instructor-led training	• Paired response, publicly shared • Small group response, publicly shared
What I Thought, What I Think	• Unlimited	• Short • Long	• Before • After	• Virtual instructor-led training • Instructor-led training • E-learning • Self-directed learning	• Individual response, private • Individual response, publicly shared • Paired response, private • Paired response, publicly shared • Small group response, private • Small response, publicly shared
Surprise, Failure, and Frustration	• Unlimited	• Medium • Long	• During • After	• Virtual instructor-led training • Instructor-led training • E-learning • Self-directed learning	• Individual response, private • Individual response, publicly shared • Small group response, private • Small group response, publicly shared

Appendix B
Tools and Templates

Visit KatrinaKennedy.com/LearningThatLasts to download digital and printable versions of these templates. You'll find these templates as well as a few filled out examples in this appendix.

- Reflecting on Your Design
- I'm Curious About . . .
- Four Corners
- Before and After
- Tell Me a Story—Storyboard
- Tell Me a Story—Story Outline
- Start, Stop, Continue
- It's a RAP
- After-Action Review
- Five Questions
- Plan, Monitor, Evaluate
- Plan, Monitor, Evaluate with Objectives
- Five Whys

Reflecting on Your Design

Use this checklist to review your design to ensure the success of your reflection activities.

Reflect on Your Design

- ☐ I've created a safe and supportive learning environment where people feel comfortable sharing their reflections and engaging in open discussions.
- ☐ I've explained the value and benefits of reflection.
- ☐ I've identified if reflection will be shared with others when I explain the activity.
- ☐ I've included structured reflection activities to encourage thinking critically about experiences, assumptions, and actions.
- ☐ I've used a variety of reflective activities with different modes of reflection (written, verbal, and visual).
- ☐ I've aligned activities with the course outcomes or objectives.
- ☐ I've provided multiple opportunities for reflection throughout the learning experience.
- ☐ I've provided clear prompts or questions to guide participants' reflection processes.
- ☐ I've provided multiple means for ongoing reflection after completion of the learning experience.
- ☐ I've included opportunities for collaborative reflection, such as group discussions or peer feedback sessions, to encourage diverse perspectives and learning from others.
- ☐ I've considered the diverse needs of people.

I'm Curious About . . .

Use this template to boost motivation at the beginning of a learning experience.

I am curious about:
because I want to find out (what/how/why):
to better understand (what/how/why):
so that I will be able to:

To increase the value of this activity, ask everyone to complete a new set of prompts at the end of the program. This time, they should reflect on the experience they just completed.

And now I know that:
means I need to:
so that I can:
My challenge will be:

I'm Curious About—Example

Beginning of the Program

I am curious about:
Methods to engage participants

because I want to find out (what/how/why):
what grabs their attention

to better understand (what/how/why):
why I'm losing people to other activities during virtual training

so that I will be able to:
lead more engaging virtual training that creates learning that lasts.

After the Program

And now I know that:
Engaging participants

means I need to:
provide meaningful activities that are relevant to their jobs

so that I can:
do less lecturing and talking.

My challenge will be:
Moving away from my old style to embrace a participant-centered approach.

Four Corners

Use this template to gain deeper insights by reflecting on your learning experience from four different perspectives.

I Liked	I Learned

I Wonder	I Will

Before and After

Use this template to create deeper insight, comparing expectations before a learning experience to what changed after.

Learning Outcomes	Before	After
		What I Knew What Changed What I Learned
		What I Knew What Changed What I Learned
		What I Knew What Changed What I Learned

Appendix B 257

Tell Me a Story—Storyboard

Use this template to outline the flow of a story. Use the blank boxes to sketch your ideas and provide descriptions in the space below. Your drawings can be simple or complex.

Description:	Description:	Description:

Description:	Description:	Description:

Description:	Description:	Description:

Tell Me a Story—Story Outline

Use this template to help you outline your story. Review the prompts in the column on the right and then write down some brief bullet points on the left side outlining your story.

The Setting • Where does your story take place?	
The Opening • How did your learning adventure begin? • What did you believe then?	
The Conflict • What obstacles did you overcome? • What hardships did you endure?	
The Resolution • What actions did you take?	
The Moral • How are you different now? • What lessons did you learn? • What do you believe now?	

Start, Stop, Continue

The Start, Stop, Continue activity is designed to help you identify specific behaviors to adjust after the training program ends.

Start	Stop	Continue

It's a RAP

Use the It's a Reflection Action Plan (RAP) template to outline what occurred during a learning experience and to identify specific actions to implement in the workplace. (See the completed example for additional guidance.)

Reflect

What are three important things you learned in [*program name*]?
1.
2.
3.

How do these three things relate to your work?
1.
2.
3.

Plan

When you return to work, what action(s) will you take based on items 1-3 above?
1.
2.
3.

By When?
1.
2.
3.

What support will you need?

Possible Obstacles

What will make it difficult to accomplish your plan?

How can you minimize these obstacles?

Checking Progress

What will you measure to check the progress of your plan?

How can [name] help support your progress after today?

It's a RAP—Example

Reflect

What are three important things you learned in [*program name*]?
1. How to write a performance goal that will be used to guide design and evaluation.
2. How to change the font on all PowerPoint slides - Design/Variance/Choose font.
3. How to write valid multiple-choice questions.
How do these three things relate to your work?
1. Writing clearer performance goals will make training more relevant, performance based, and learner centered.
2. Saves time updating PowerPoint decks, more accessible with sans serif font.
3. Better questions will measure learning more effectively.

Plan

When you return to work, what actions will you take based on items 1-3 above?
1. Write a performance goal for all new training I'm designing
2. Streamline the fonts in the PowerPoint deck I was provided.
3. Review my questions before an upcoming training program.
By When?
1. December 14
2. November 5
3. March 14
What support will you need?
• Time from my manager to make updates. • Agreement with my manager to revise multiple-choice questions

Possible Obstacles

What will make it difficult to accomplish your plan?
Conflicting priorities/time to complete the plan.

How can you minimize these obstacles?
Work with management on priorities and adjust my schedule as needed.

Checking Progress

What will you measure to check the progress of your plan?
- Number of classes with clear performance goals. - Completion of font changes by my deadline. - Two peer reviewed questions written.

How can Katrina help support your progress after today?
Send me a check-in email around January 7.

After-Action Review

Use the After-Action Review to help support change in behavior after a learning experience. (See the completed example on the next page for additional guidance.)

After-Action Review Focus

1. What did you expect to happen?

2. What actually happened?

3. Why was there a difference between what was expected and what happened?

4. What can you change next time?

After-Action Review—Completed Example

After-Action Review Focus: Emerging Leaders Program

1. What did you expect to happen?
Gain tools, techniques, and skills to lead a diverse group of employees. A lot of listening and perhaps some videos.
2. What actually happened?
Highly interactive, hands-on practice including role-plays. Spent much of the time thinking about whether a leadership role was the desired path. Surprised by the amount of reflection but saw the benefit by the end of the program.
3. Why was there a difference between what was expected and what happened?
There wasn't a clear picture provided of the structure of the program. Marketing focused on the objectives and not the process. The hybrid structure was mentioned but the balance between individual work, virtual sessions, and in-person time wasn't made clear.
4. What can you change next time?
Ask more questions up front and suggest future programs provide a clearer outline of the structure.

Five Questions

Use this template to think critically about an experience through answering five journalistic-style questions.

What have you learned about [*insert your topic*]?
When will you use what you've learned?
Where will you use what you've learned?
How will you use what you've learned?
Why will you use what you've learned?
Bonus question: When will you review your responses? (Set a specific date.)

Plan, Monitor, Evaluate

Use this template to plan for your learning experience, monitor its progress, and evaluate your results.

Plan: *What I Plan to Learn*	Monitor: *What I've learned*	Evaluate: *How I'll use what I've learned*

Plan, Monitor, Evaluate With Objectives

Use this template to plan for your learning experience based on the learning objectives, monitor your progress, and evaluate your results.

Objective	Monitor: What I've learned	Evaluate: How I'll use what I've learned	Evaluate: How I'll Use What I've Learned
1			
2			
3			
4			
5			

Five Whys

Use this template to examine and question a belief or insight you've gained.

I want to:

Why?

Why?

Why?

Why?

Why?

References

Amabile, T., and S. Kramer. 2011. "Four Reasons to Keep a Work Diary." *Harvard Business Review*, April 27. hbr.org/2011/04/four-reasons-to-keep-a-work-di.

Armstrong, P.B. 2020. *Stories and the Brain: The Neuroscience of Narrative*. Johns Hopkins University Press.

Bailey, J.R., and S. Rehman. 2022. "Don't Underestimate the Power of Self-Reflection." *Harvard Business Review*, March 4. hbr.org/2022/03/dont-underestimate-the-power-of-self-reflection.

Biech, E. 2016. *The Art and Science of Training*. ATD Press.

Biel, D., and N. Bunzeck. 2019. "Novelty Before or After Word Learning Does Not Affect Subsequent Memory Performance." *Frontiers in Psychology* 10. doi.org/10.3389/fpsyg.2019.01379.

Binnewies, C., S. Sonnentag, and E.J. Mojza. 2009. "Feeling Recovered and Thinking About the Good Sides of One's Work." *Journal of Occupational Health Psychology* 14(3): 243–56. doi.org/10.1037/a0014933.

Brown, P.C., H.L. Roediger, and M.A. McDaniel. 2014. *Make It Stick: The Science of Successful Learning*. Belknap Press.

Di Stefano, G., F. Gino, G.P. Pisano, and B.R. Staats. 2023. "Learning by Thinking: How Reflection Can Spur Progress Along the Learning Curve." *Harvard Business School NOM Unit Working Paper* No. 14-093. ssrn.com/abstract=2414478.

Ditta, A.S., C.M. Strickland-Hughes, C. Cheung, and R. Wu. 2020. "Exposure to Information Increases Motivation to Learn More." *Learning and Motivation* 72:101668. doi.org/10.1016/j.lmot.2020.101668.

Dorgo, A. 2024. "We've Been Fed a Lie: Practice Doesn't Make Perfect." Irregular Letter, August 30. anamariadorgo.substack.com/p/weve-been-fed-a-lie-practice-doesnt.

Doumont, J.-L. 2002. "Magical Numbers: The Seven-Plus-or-Minus-Two Myth." *IEEE Transactions on Professional Communication* 45(2): 123–27. doi.org/10.1109/TPC.2002.1003695.

Edidin, R. 2013. "Comedy Gold: Reading Your Teenage Diary for a Live Audience." *Wired*, November 5. wired.com/2013/11/mortified-nation-documentary.

Edmondson, A. 2023. *Right Kind of Wrong: The Science of Failing Well*. Simon Element.

Edmondson, A.C., and P. Hugander. 2021. "4 Steps to Boost Psychological Safety at Your Workplace." *Harvard Business Review*, June 22. hbr.org/2021/06/4-steps-to-boost-psychological-safety-at-your-workplace.

Ellis, S., R. Mendel, and M. Nir. 2006. "Learning from Successful and Failed Experience: The Moderating Role of Kind of After-Event Review." *Journal of Applied Psychology* 91: 669–80. pubmed.ncbi.nlm.nih.gov/16737362.

Fernandes, M.A., J.D. Wammes, and M.E. Meade. 2018. "The Surprisingly Powerful Influence of Drawing on Memory." *Current Directions in Psychological Science* 27(5): 302–8. doi.org/10.1177/0963721418755385.

Fletcher, A., P.B. Cline, and M. Hoffman. 2023. "A Better Approach to After-Action Reviews." *Harvard Business Review*, January 12. hbr.org/2023/01/a-better-approach-to-after-action-reviews.

Hall, M.J. 2023. "Reflecting on Reflection." ATD Blog, February 17. td.org/content/atd-blog/reflecting-on-reflection.

Huggett, C. 2024. *The Virtual Training Guidebook*, 2nd ed. ATD Press.

Jose, J., and M.M. Joseph. 2018. "Imagery: Its Effects and Benefits on Sports Performance and Psychological Variables: A Review Study." *International Journal of Physiology, Nutrition and Physical Education* 3(2): 190–3. journalofsports.com/pdf/2018/vol3issue2/PartE/3-2-41-617.pdf.

Kahneman, D. 2011. *Thinking, Fast and Slow*. Farrar, Straus and Giroux.

Kapp, K. 2022. "Dimensions of Wisdom." L&D Easter Eggs, December 20. linkedin.com/pulse/dimensions-wisdom-karl-kapp.

Kirschner, F., F. Paas, and P.A. Kirschner. 2009. "A Cognitive Load Approach to Collaborative Learning: United Brains for Complex Tasks." *Educational Psychology Review* 21:31–42. doi.org/10.1007/S10648-008-9095-2.

Kolb, D.A. 1984. *Experiential Learning: Experience as the Source of Learning and Development*. Prentice-Hall.

Kross, E., M. Ong, and O. Ayduk. 2023. "Self-Reflection at Work: Why It Matters and How to Harness Its Potential and Avoid Its Pitfalls." *Annual Review of Organizational Psychology and Organizational Behavior* 10:109–34. doi.org/10.1146/annurev-orgpsych-031921-024406.

Kross, E., Ö. Ayduk, and W. Mischel. 2005. "When Asking 'Why' Does Not Hurt: Distinguishing Rumination From Reflective Processing of Negative Emotions." *Psychological Science* 16(9): 709–15. doi.org/10.1111/j.1467-9280.2005.01600.x.

Kurdi, B., A.J. Diaz, C.A. Wilmuth, M.C. Friedman, and M.R. Banaji. 2018. "Variations in the Relationship Between Memory Confidence and Memory Accuracy: The Effects of Spontaneous Accessibility, List Length, Modality, and Complexity." *Psychology of Consciousness: Theory, Research, and Practice* 5(1): 3–28. doi.org/10.1037/cns0000117.

Lee, J.Y., J. Donkers, H. Jarodzka, G. Sellenraad, Tjitske J.E. Faber, and J.V. van Merriënboer. 2024. "The Effects of Reflective Pauses on Performance in Simulation Training." *Simulation in Healthcare: Journal of the Society for Simulation in Healthcare* 19(2): 82–9. doi.org/10.1097/SIH.0000000000000729.

Mercier, S. 2025. *Design for All Learners: Create Accessible and Inclusive Learning Experiences*. ATD Press.

McCabe, G., and T. Thejll-Madsen. 2024. "Reflection Toolkit." University of Edinburgh. ed.ac.uk/reflection.

Moon, J.A. 2013. *Reflection in Learning and Professional Development: Theory and Practice*. Routledge.

Pagan, A. 2018. "A Brief History of Gothic Horror." New York Public Library, October 18. nypl.org/blog/2018/10/18/brief-history-gothic-horror.

Quinn, C.N. 2018. *Millennials, Goldfish, and Other Training Misconceptions*. ATD Press.

Ragan, T. 2024. "The Power of Reflection: How Thinking Improves Learning & Performance - ft. Giada Di Stefano." Video. February 19. youtube.com/watch?v=IRDhHb987Wc.

Renner, B., G. Wesiak, V. Pammer-Schindler, et al. 2019. "Computer-Supported Reflective Learning: How Apps Can Foster Reflection at Work." *Behaviour & Information Technology* 39(2): 167–87. doi.org/10.1080/0144929X.2019.1595726.

Ribiero, L.C., Mamede, A. Moura, E.M. de Brito, R.M.D. de Faria, and H. Schmidt. 2018. "Effect of Reflection on Medical Student's Situational Interest: An Experimental Study." *Medical Education* 52: 48-496. doi.org/10.11111/medu.13491.

Rigolizzo, Michele, and Zhu Zhu. 2020. "Motivating Reflection Habits and Raising Employee Awareness of Learning." *Department of Management Faculty Scholarship and Creative Works*, no. 43. digitalcommons.montclair.edu/management-facpubs/43.

Roberts, B.R.T., and J.D. Wammes. 2021. "Drawing and Memory: Using Visual Production to Alleviate Concreteness Effects." *Psychonomic Bulletin & Review* 28:259–67. doi.org/10.3758/s13423-020-01804-w.

Roediger, H.L., and A.C. Butler. 2011. "The Critical Role of Retrieval Practice in Long-Term Retention." *Trends in Cognitive Sciences* 15(1): 20–7. doi.org/10.1016/j.tics.2010.09.003.

Shank, P. 2021. *Write Better Multiple-Choice Questions to Assess Learning*. Published by the author.

Stolovitch, H.D., and E.J. Keeps. 2002. *Telling Ain't Training*. ASTD Press.

Tipton, S. 2023. "Create Drip Feeds to Revolutionize Learning Retention." *TD*, December 1. td.org/content/td-magazine/create-drip-feeds-to-revolutionize-learning-retention.

University of Cambridge Libraries. n.d. Reflective Practice Toolkit. libguides.cam.ac.uk/reflectivepracticetoolkit/models.

Van Hooydonk, S. 2022. *The Workplace Curiosity Manifesto*. New Degree Press.

Yang, C., B. Sun, R. Potts, R. Yu, L. Luo, and D.R. Shanks. 2020. "Do Working Memory Capacity and Test Anxiety Modulate the Beneficial Effects of Testing on New Learning?" *Journal of Experimental Psychology: Applied* 26(4): 724–38. doi.org/10.1037/xap0000278.

Zhang, T., T. Kim, A.W. Brooks, F. Gino, and M.I. Norton. 2014. "A 'Present' for the Future: The Unexpected Value of Rediscovery." *Psychological Science* 25(10): 1851–60.

About the Author

Katrina Kennedy, known as the "trainer's trainer," is a facilitator, speaker, and author with more than 28 years of experience in learning and development. She has helped thousands of subject matter experts design and deliver engaging learning experiences in a variety of industries. When she's not facilitating you can find her wandering in her vegetable garden or playing board games with her family. She shares training insights and ideas at katrinakennedy.com.

About ATD

The Association for Talent Development (ATD) is the world's largest association dedicated to those who develop talent in organizations. Serving a global community of members, customers, and international business partners in more than 100 countries, ATD champions the importance of learning and training by setting standards for the talent development profession.

Our customers and members work in public and private organizations in every industry sector. Since ATD was founded in 1943, the talent development field has expanded significantly to meet the needs of global businesses and emerging industries. Through the Talent Development Capability Model, education courses, certifications and credentials, memberships, industry-leading events, research, and publications, we help talent development professionals build their personal, professional, and organizational capabilities to meet new business demands with maximum impact and effectiveness.

One of the cornerstones of ATD's intellectual foundation, ATD Press offers insightful and practical information on talent development, training, and professional growth. ATD Press publications are written by industry thought leaders and offer anyone who works with adult learners the best practices, academic theory, and guidance necessary to move the profession forward.

We invite you to join our community. Learn more at **td.org**.

www.ingramcontent.com/pod-product-compliance
Ingram Content Group UK Ltd.
Pitfield, Milton Keynes, MK11 3LW, UK
UKHW062304141125
465102UK00020B/139